OVER THE EDGE AND BACK

TRUE STORIES OF 40 TEENS

WHO BECAME WINNERS

IN LIFE'S TOUGHEST BATTLES

JOE WHITE

Questar Publishers, Inc.

OVER THE EDGE AND BACK

CONTENTS

The Largest Teen Fraternity 7

1. Danger! 11

2. The Truth about Falling 19

3. Where the Bullets Fly 25

4. Great Sexpectations 35

5. The Sting of Rejection 49

6. Sweet Tarts 61

7. The Last Word Is Good 65

8. Out of the Pit 73

9. When God Is at His Best 87

10. At the End of the End 101

11. Knowing the Love 111

12. More Out of Life 121

13. Follow the Star 129

14. Always on the Line 139

15. Time to Declare War 149

    First and Ten (for your daily Quiet Times) 161

    Topical Index.. 195

The more than forty brave people whose stories are told in their own words in this book are all young friends of mine. Most are in high school. A few are in college or are recent college graduates.

We didn't put any makeup on these true-life "school pictures." These stories are personal and obedient to candid reality (only names have been changed). We knew it was time to sweep away the sand and give a clear view— from their perspective—of their pitfalls, their failures...and their climb to the top of the mountain.

If you've ever wanted to see what it looks like after a dark-side journey to the peak, get out your climbing ropes and your backpack... and let my friends be your guide.

THE LARGEST TEEN FRATERNITY

L ori Anne was a petite 14-year-old freshman when she slipped sheepishly into the back row of our sorta hyper Youth Club. I will never forget the moment I first saw her. The patch over her left eye and the searching scowl on her forehead reached out and grabbed my heart. The kids told me after Club that Lori had facial cancer. Her first surgery necessitated the removal of her eye and other tissue from her face.

She came back week after week to the Club. We began to talk. Lori taught me that the trivial things of life don't really matter anymore, when you are not yet fifteen and your final days are falling wildly through the hourglass of time like sand in a desert storm.

Lori wanted to touch the eternal, so we talked together and dug together through the disappointment and pain and into the dimension of true reality—the reality that God had a plan for Lori that was a whole lot bigger than life on this planet. Lori was like an angel unaware of her special mission. She asked for the Savior, and He flowed into her heart with a peace and assurance that transcended her medical plight.

Chemical and radiation treatment in the next two years failed to restore Lori's wellness. Her body was dying, just as the tender shoot of new spiritual life broke through the soil of her eternal soul. As the sun was setting on Lori Anne's physical life, a sunrise of supernatural understanding peeked over the horizon of her heart, sparkling in her eye and in a smile that left a lasting impression on everyone. None of us will ever be the same...none of us that is, who knew Lori.

A few weeks before Lori died, she lay quietly in her hospital bed surrounded by balloons, flowers, teddy bears, and the care of some of the world's best physicians. They, too, had fallen in love with Lori, but now it was time to tell this 16-year old saint goodbye.

"Lori." The gentle voice of the chief surgeon broke the silence. "We've tried everything we know. It isn't working. We can't do any more. You're going to die soon, sweet girl..."

Lori looked steadily into his eyes and spoke softly. "Don't feel bad. I'm not going to die when the medicine runs out. I'll die when Jesus calls me home."

Lori had tucked a verse from the Psalms into the deepest crevice of her soul. She quietly quoted it: "I have known you; I have carved you in the palm of my hand." Lori and her Master were so close—so very close together.

Lori was flown home to spend her last few days with friends and family. I took a celebrity friend of mine to her bedside to sing to her and give her a special moment to remember. (Coincidentally, she had seen him just the night before on television.) Like everyone else who visited Lori Anne, the TV star departed having received more than he gave.

Two days later, a priest visited Lori. He commented on the celebrity's visit: "I'll bet that was the time of your life!"

"What's a celebrity," Lori answered, "when you're going to see Jesus in a week?"

Five days later, the curtain was raised between her life on this planet and life in the full presence of her beloved Savior. A minute before she died, Lori whispered softly to her mother, "Mom, I want you to know Jesus the way I do."

God's grace, as promised, was abundant in Lori Anne's sixteen years. She knew that life wasn't measured in length of stay here, but in the quality and depth of her friendship with the Man named Jesus.

Lori's faith never quit. As her circumstances grew worse, she pressed on harder. Like a well-trained athlete, she hit the peak of her life in the final lap. Testing became triumph.

Lori was a member of the largest teenage fraternity in the world: a brotherhood and sisterhood of pain, disappointment, tragedy, rejection, and misunderstanding. As I've spoken with thousands of kids across America, I've never met a young person who wasn't a member of this club during at least part of his or her junior high, high school, or college days.

And as times get crazier, there is infinitely more hurt in this age group than in the decades before. Every time I speak to a high school or youth group or listen to the throbbing heartbeat of a searching kid, I'm convinced again that we are in a youth war—a Vietnam or Persian Gulf for kids, right here on American soil. The fighters are 14, 17, maybe 19 years old.

You may be one of the warriors today...or perhaps it was yesterday...or it could be tomorrow. The battlefield might be alcohol, or a car accident that caused the death of a friend, or a disease, or dyslexia, or a birth defect. It could be a cruel father, a broken home, a deep scar of guilt, never-ending loneliness, depression that dogs you like a bloodhound, or suicidal feelings. Your battlefield might be the heat of a pusher, the relentless fear of being overweight, a group of peers who reject you and gossip about you at school, a facial feature that makes looking into the mirror a dreaded moment each day, a girlfriend who calls it quits, an unfaithful boyfriend, a potential athletic career devastated by an injury.

If you've ever cried yourself to sleep or wondered if you'd ever see the sunshine again, get ready in this book to meet some new friends who are walking in your shoes. They come from coast to coast. They include the rich and the poor and every race. I believe you'll find a home with us and I hope you'll discover a new understanding and a giant dose of love. I want this book to be a cloud-buster, a soft shoulder for your tears, and a map that shows the way from the canyon floor to the mountaintop.

You see, I too grew up in that canyon, and cut my teeth on question marks and feelings of worthlessness. But caring friends and family members helped set my feet on the highway leading to real happiness. That's why I never grow weary of taking an outstretched hand and helping someone else find the way.

So join my young friends and me as the following pages unfold. Let us prepare you for tomorrow's bumps, heal you from yesterday's bruises, and erase your fears of the troublesome times in which we live.

JOE WHITE
Branson, Missouri

1

DANGER!

Ostriches stick their head in the sand when they sense trouble. Their population diminishes daily, The beautiful birds would flourish if somehow we could only tell them: "Look up! Examine the danger! React!"

NEVER AGAIN

On a cold Monday in October, as I lay in the emergency room hooked up to a heart machine, I thought back over the last thirteen years of my life. And I thought about the last thirteen hours. I had shot up $245 worth of coke, and thirteen hours later I thought I was having a heart attack. After I called 911, I had to tell the paramedic why my chest hurt. As soon as I did, my case was no longer a heart attack. It was a drug overdose!

Now as I lay there, I prayed, "God, take my life." Ah, but how He loved me! "No, you won't die," He was telling me. "Learn from your life and help someone."

It was peer pressure that caused me to light my first joint. I was in college—big girl on campus. I was taken in by the we-love-God-and-dope crowd: Go to church, then get high and see the beauty in the mountains. I had one friend who told me it was all wrong: One drug leads to another, she would say. (That girl was right!) My response was always,

"It will never happen to me," or "What's wrong with it?" or even, "Christ drank a little wine; it's the same high."

After the weed came the beer and Seagram's 7, because soon the weed wasn't enough. I left college and moved to the big city. In between drugs and liquor, I tried to keep Christ in my life, but somehow Satan would overthrow my faith. There I would be again, smoking dope.

I met some new friends who said they had a high for me I'd *never* forget. It was a rainy night, I remember. We had to go downtown to the inner city to get the dope. I didn't really know where we were or what was going on. I was scared, but they kept telling me, "Get with it. Grow up." One friend went to the door, put the money in a slot, and waited three or four minutes. The dope came out the slot.

We went home to the basement to cook up the dope. We drew it up in a syringe. I put the tie on my arm, closed my eyes, and let my friends send me to paradise. I don't remember much more about that night. I knew I felt good, but I also felt a little guilty. But I didn't care, and I opened every door Satan wanted me to. Before I knew it—I don't even know how it happened—I had a habit. Addiction, I learned, is when your mind no longer has control; your body takes over, and Satan runs your life.

Soon my friends no longer wanted to get me high; now they wanted me to get *them* high. They were already down and out, but I still had a job. So on pay day we would all make the trip to the city. I was shooting T's and blues, then perluden, then heroin, then coke.

I was hooked on coke. Do you know how much coke you can shoot in one day? Some of my friends could spend $700 a night. I couldn't hold a job (I lost two good ones), and I didn't know how I would get the money to get high. Guess what Satan said? *Steal. Sell everything you own. Lie.*

At this point it had been eleven years since my good friend told me one drug leads to another. I was still convinced I'd never let them get me down. I didn't want to be around people who wanted to help me, and most of all, I didn't want to admit I needed help.

I would have sold my soul for dope. I made deals with the devil to get it. I was nothing but a big dope-head. I lied to my best friends. I made people hate me.

Not only did I have a drug problem; I also had to have a drink every day. I didn't even know who I was.

I thought back to how happy and together my life used to be when Christ was in my life. I decided it was time to get help. I went to the clinic, got the dope out of my life, and was clean for six months. No hard drugs… just a little weed. No hard liquor… just a little beer. Life was going well. I felt I had regained control.

Then it happened! The world fell out from under me. Satan said, *I have something to make you feel good. Come on, it's just what you need.* There it was! I was back on the drugs, and drinking again to forget.

But on that cold October Monday, I put the needle in my arm for the last time. As I lay in the emergency room, Christ came in and said to me, "I love you. And if you live in Me, I will care for you. If you live in Satan, you will surely die."

The doctor walked in. "We want to admit you to a drug clinic," he said. I promised I'd never do it again. The doctor asked how I could be sure; did I know what coke does to a person? My answer was yes. I had lived it for years: You quit caring, you quit loving, and then you want to die.

From that moment, I let Christ take charge of my life, something I had never done. There were people who tried to get me to surrender to Christ—my friend in college, my family—but I'd never listened.

The answer to my problem was this: FACE IT, DON'T FIGHT IT; GOD WILL FIX IT.

It's been only two months since I've been clean. But there won't be any more drugs in my life. Drugs kill. Drugs are out. Drugs run *you;* you don't run them. When you want to try one high, there's always one that's better. One high leads to another. Is it worth it? If I could help one person stay off drugs, I would feel totally blessed.

It's funny: All the friends I used to get high with don't come around anymore. But the one Friend who waited for me was always there. And when I went to the hospital, my dope friends weren't there. The only friends I had in the world were Jesus and one faithful Christian friend who told me that one drug leads to another. Had I listened to my friend thirteen years ago, I would not have memories today of dope, alcohol, and depression. I would have good memories of a normal life and of doing good instead of evil.

God is my strength. When temptation comes, I pray, "In Jesus' name, I command you to leave, Satan." Satan is everything evil. So why would we want to live as he does?

My Christian friend gave me a poem. (She lost her own brother to an overdose of heroin—after he started out smoking pot!) Read this poem by an unknown author a couple of times, and think about it:

So, little man, you've grown tired of grass,
LSD, goofballs, cocaine and hash.
And someone pretending to be a good friend
says, "Let me introduce you to Miss Heroin."
Well, honey, before you fool with me,
let me inform you of how it will be.
For I will seduce you and make you a slave;
I've sent men much stronger than you to a grave.
You think you could never become a disgrace,
end up an addict to poppyseed and waste,
so you'll start inhaling me some afternoon
and take me in your arm very soon!

And once I enter, drip down in your veins,
your cravings will drive you nearly insane.
You'll swindle your mother, and just for a buck
you'll turn into something vile and corrupt.
You'll mug and steal for my narcotic charm,
you'll feel contentment when I'm in your arm.
The day you realize the monster you've grown
you'll solemnly promise to leave me alone.
Well, if you think you've got the mystical knack,
then try getting me, Miss Heroin, off your back.
You vomit, you cramp, you get tied in a knot,
your jangling nerves screaming for one more shot.
The hot sweat, the cold chill, the withdrawing pain
can only be stopped by my little white grain.
No other way! There's no need to look;
for deep down inside, you know you are hooked.
You desperately run to your pusher, and then
you welcome me back to your arm once again.
And once you return, as I have foretold,
you give me your body, and give up your soul.
You give up your morals, your conscience, your heart,
and you will be mine till death do us part!

IT'S UP TO US

Last year was the first year my peers really started getting into things. Yeah, I'm sure some of them did it earlier, but it didn't show up until eighth grade. Some drank, smoked, and were involved in drugs, and others were getting involved with Satan. It started scaring me when I first saw my good Christian friends getting interested in things like tarot cards. A girl brought out a set of them one day at school during lunch. Most of my friends didn't realize what they were and crowded around, wanting to play. When I told them what they were, they didn't care. It really upset me to see how innocent people could get involved in things like that and not even realize it while it's happening.

That day during study hall I wanted to get my thoughts and feelings out, so I wrote a song. Here it is:

Things happen in this world today that tear God far apart.
The only place He still remains is deep in Christians' hearts.
The ouija board, and werewolves too, are all Satanic things;
people don't seem to realize the darkness that they bring.
It's not only the lost people in these present days
who get involved in so many bad Satanic ways.
It's believers just like me and you
who need a light to show them, too,
to block out all the wrong things and only do what's right.
Quick, before this earth becomes a terrible world of fright!
The very few who still remain,
who are not crazy, who aren't insane,
are the only true hope for this dying earth—
the only ones to set it straight, to give it new birth.
It's up to us to stand up for our God today,
to make the earth change its course, and head the right way.

EDDIE'S STORY

"SEX-CESS"

In fifth grade I had two friends who would bring pages ripped from their fathers' pornographic magazines over to my house. We'd look at the pictures and laugh, having no idea that those pictures would linger in our minds forever. My parents didn't care who I spent time with, so my friends and I would listen to "everyday" (sexually explicit) music and go to "popular" (sexually explicit) movies. Our minds became what every kid's mind becomes who isn't careful what he watches or listens to. We couldn't wait to make out with a girl. Success was spelled "sex-cess."

When we started going out in high school, I got a girl-friend, Peggy, and we went out for about six months. Although we didn't go all the way, we did everything else. Little did I know that petting is such a trap for sex.

Peggy and I broke up because of the sexual pressure we

put into our relationship. Peggy had gone all the way before, but I hadn't. It was all a big mess.

Then I met a girl named Angie. Since Peggy and I had done almost everything, it was easy to rationalize heavy petting with Angie. I really thought I loved Angie, so to make it a more meaningful relationship than the one I'd had with Peggy, we decided to go all the way. For Angie it was giving up her virginity. Wow! That was so wrong of me. Angie and I somehow fell out of love and both of us moved on to other people. After having sex with Angie, I had sex with four other girls over the next four years. You always hear how the girl gets all the blame and all the guilt. Well, I am living proof that that's a big lie. It still hurts me to this day, and I regard what happened with Angie to be the biggest mistake I ever made in my life.

After my last girlfriend broke up with me, I was hurt badly, and a friend was there to lead me into a relationship with Christ. Although I had grown up going to church, I had never made a personal commitment to the Lord, and really only went to church because my parents made me.

Now it was much different. I began to see girls through different eyes. I cared for their sexual purity. I cared for mine as well. I guess you could say that Jesus gave me "sex-cess" because He helped me overcome my weakness, and He gave me a desire to wait for sex until I get married some day.

NATHAN'S STORY

MIND BATTLE

I just returned from the dry-out hospital. I guess free-basing cocaine was just too much for me. The music I listened to attracted me to it. My favorite groups were Slayer and Dokken. I knew I was in trouble when I got into a

OVER THE EDGE AND BACK

small seance. We drew a pentagon on the floor and put candles on all five points of the star. We had our ouija board in the middle and we started doing stupid things. We asked the ouija board its name. It said to go to the TV set. The name appeared on the TV set. We asked the ouija board, and it said "Yes." The name was "Unrested Soul." It got creepy, so I started smoking dope.

We vandalized stuff too, and I got dangerous. If someone touched me, I'd beat him up. My eyes would cross. My mom and sister would hide when they saw me getting angry. If I wasn't doing drugs, I was having sex. It was a hell —an experience I don't want to go through again.

The groups I listened to get all their songs from horror movies. They tell how to kill people. They make fun of a preacher and how he says, "Jesus saves." I really got into their music.

I was attracted to blood and guts and gore. One night I was doing a cocaine deal. We jumped the guy and tied him to a fence. We got a red-hot iron cross and branded him. Then we beat him up, and laughed and laughed. That's what the songs were all about. I was fourteen. It happens. I learned from it, but I wish I hadn't learned that way.

I'm scared to make friends now because they only relapse and get back into drugs, and you have to look for other friends, and then *they* relapse. I'm scared to get close. My best friend just froze his lungs sniffing butane, and died. Another friend is still in the hospital.

You've got to respect your mind, man. What goes into it begins to own it and soon it makes decisions for you that you didn't want to make. Music is a trap. What sounds so cool and looks so cool almost wrecked my life.

I'm lucky to be out of it now—so lucky to be alive!

2

THE TRUTH ABOUT FALLING

From the day a baby takes his first step from his safe, comfortable crib, he begins a journey of adventure—of failure, recovery, success—a journey that continues until he leaves this planet.

My four kids' childhood photos (probably like your own) show them with noticeable scratches and bruises on elbows and knees and faces from many perilous trips on the stairways up and down our cliffside home. They fell, but they got up again.

Now their wounds are mostly on the inside, from teenage struggles that wait around every dark corner. They fall, and they continue to get up.

After all, pulling yourself up from disaster can give you confidence, and more. My grandmom is 96. She falls daily. She still smiles when she pulls herself up in a nearby chair. She's strong, dignified, and a blessing to everyone who enters her home.

Maybe you know a lot about falling, just as so many of my friends do...

STEVE'S STORY

I DIDN'T THINK I COULD LOVE ANYONE

My personal battle began when I was four years old, and my mom with her four kids moved to a new town many miles away from my dad. I didn't fully understand for six years that divorce was actually the reason for the move.

The sense of loss has been mysteriously haunting. A step-dad came into the picture a few years later. He brought years of emotional abuse into my life. I felt lots of hatred and anger during my early teenage years.

As I got into high school, a very wonderful thing happened to me: I asked Christ into my life one Sunday morning. I had some good Christian friends and a great youth group that supported my decision and gave me strength during those tedious years.

In my freshman year of college I began to slip and fall from my faith. Drinking was a huge downfall for me. Alcohol led me into a pattern of living that almost destroyed me. I ran from God and deceived myself into thinking I wasn't worthy to accept all God had for me. As I searched for identity, I decided to join the Marines, to give me a reason for existing. My heart was as black as coal and as hard as a diamond. I believed my soul was a stranger to God Almighty.

During that time in my life I didn't think I could love anyone. After I was commissioned as an officer, the Lord brought a very special person into my life. Wendy personified everything I had turned my back on, so I lashed out at her as well. Even though I blew the relationship, the Lord gave her a special place of lasting respect in my heart. She never stopped encouraging me spiritually with birthday cards, Christmas cards, and other creative ways of saying, "I believe in you." She is truly an amazing person.

As I've struggled through my spiritual desert in the Marine Corps, it has been one step forward and two steps back. The potential to witness here is astounding, but spiritually I felt defeated. I kept pursuing God. There is something about being ready to go into a battle face to face with real bullets (perhaps worse) that brings a soldier into a very real, very honest point of understanding what really matters about life on this planet.

Wendy kept encouraging me. It's amazing what one strong Christian friend can do for you! She never compromised herself in any way for me. She never let me take her one step back. She cared for me as a friend...not a boyfriend. (Never underestimate the power of friendship. Just one person who is willing to stand in the gap for Jesus Christ can make all the difference in the world to a lost soldier. A girl who is strong in the Lord can change the cold heart of even a Marine like me!)

Today I believe I am standing on the threshold of God's plan for my life. I only regret that there was so much time wasted—so much time, and so many people I could have influenced for Christ.

But I no longer fear that I'll ever fall again as I did before. I'm committed to being God's witness. As I read God's Word and a book by Tim Hansel called *Holy Sweat,* I have a guidebook to remind me of my responsibility as a Christian to the people around me.

PREGNANT WITH HONOR

A pregnancy test can be the longest test in history—all two minutes of it. And if you're not married, it's a breathless wait. I really found out the meaning of the saying, "I saw my life flash before my eyes." Mine did in those two minutes.

It was the start of a new college semester and I was just a year away from graduation. I lived on Greek Row and had lots of friends. I had just ended a two-year romance, and I had a promising future lined up in a management position with a major airline. There I was, sitting with a nurse, and desperately looking for the signs of a negative pregnancy test. The signs didn't come; she confirmed I was pregnant.

How was I going to tell my parents? My grandparents? They were all conservative, Christian, and proud of my accomplishments. Other members of my family had expressed their fears about my lifestyle. Now I was proving them right.

I was sick morning, noon and night for five months. I couldn't keep anything down. I had to leave many classes praying I'd make it to the bathroom on time. If I saw someone I knew in the bathroom, I'd comment about having the flu. Walking across campus seemed like a marathon.

I wanted the semester to be over, and yet I didn't know where I was going to live once it ended. (I hadn't lived at home for years.) I confided in a group of friends, and they said they'd stand by me. (Only two did.)

The spring-break trip I helped plan went on without me. I was too sick and it seemed meaningless. I had stopped smoking and drinking.

My bosses at work were very understanding of my problem in that they weren't judgmental. Two of them told me I was going to ruin my life if I didn't have an abortion. Even a family member said to me more than once, "Are you sure you don't want to have an abortion?" Another said, "How could you be so stupid?" It was my father. I never asked him exactly what he meant.

The loneliness and despair were indescribable. However, I knew that abortion was wrong. I had no idea how I was going to make it, but I knew this wasn't the baby's fault. My Christian background and God Himself sustained me. It would have been so easy to believe the "tissue theory," instead of the fact that *life* begins at the moment of conception. I also knew that college life, wonderful jobs, and "best friends" would come and go; down the road they wouldn't seem so important. But a baby? A baby is a lifetime of importance.

So I decided to stay pregnant. Soon people on campus heard of my pregnancy. Going to eat in the Greek Cafe meant being surrounded by people staring. I couldn't even force myself to get up for a salad or dessert because I couldn't stand the stares.

At my spring formal it was "Dear Abby" night. Girls stood waiting to talk to me. One confessed having had a high school abortion, and how much she regretted it. She had kept her secret from everyone, including her closest friend. I learned there is no one who's had an abortion who doesn't carry scars. One girl I knew had to quit school, and had a breakdown. Two others now know the forgiveness of Christ but still have emotional pain. One told me it took her almost a year after her abortion before reality hit her: She said she woke up one day and said, "I should have a baby. Where is my baby?"

I want the world to know there are ways around abortion. There is no family, financial, or emotional situation that warrants it. There are Crisis Pregnancy Centers all over the country. (If only I had known about them back then; I didn't get counseling until my sixth month, and it was a tremendous help.)

Today my daughter is happy, healthy, and athletic, and she excels in school. At times I watch her with such awe and overwhelming emotion. When she receives awards at school, I'm the mom who's looking up at the ceiling trying to get those tears back in her head, only to blow it at the last minute by jumping up to get that picture.

Then there are the precious times when she rides her bike next to me when I jog, or when we hike in the park before breakfast. And there's the unforgettable time when she was two and walked down the aisle in front of me at my wedding, and later joined my husband and me at the altar for a family prayer. And now I get to hear her laughing with her brother and sister.

I have never regretted my decision. Times weren't easy, and sometimes were agonizing; but those times seem insignificant when compared to my daughter. The joy is indescribable. I am so blessed and honored to have her.

3

WHERE
THE BULLETS FLY

The best way to keep from getting shot in a war is to stay away from flying bullets. Without a doubt the worst hurts in the teenage and college years come from mistakes with sex. I've seen more tears and broken hearts result from going down the wrong road sexually than from any other hazard—by far. The sexual skirmish is where the bullets are flying.

After almost twenty years, I adore my wife more than ever before. Kissing her has never been better. Sex is supposed to be like that too. It is a God-invented wedding gift for a husband and wife to share with each other (and only with each other) that sets marriage apart from every other relationship on planet earth.

When it comes to sex, everything from kissing to intercourse is tender, tender ground. As thousands of kids in America every day are finding out, once you kiss someone, that relationship takes on a whole new dimension. Someone is probably going to get hurt eventually. The further you go, the worse the pain. It's a terrible way to gamble.

TV shows, car and beer commercials (which mostly sell sex, with the product thrown in on the side), magazines, music, and movies have gotten us brainwashed into believing that everyone is having sex with whoever comes along, and that sex in any circumstance is fun. If you're not sexually involved with someone, so the myth goes, there's something wrong with you. *Mademoiselle* magazine labels it "The Joy of Sex Appeal."

I've counseled thousands and thousands of teenagers on the subject, and I promise you....nothing could be further from the truth! Listen to their cries:

A 19-year-old college freshman—

After I met Bobby, I trusted him to know how far we could go without making love. He was in the driver's seat. He was also insecure; he would tell me over and over how he loved me, how he was sure I didn't love him as much as he loved me. It was then that I set out to prove it. I was his—110% his. The first time we made love, I had no idea what was going on. Afterward, he didn't speak. I've never hated myself more.

Sex became an everyday occurrence. My only fear was losing Bobby. I was going to do anything I could to hang onto him. Slowly we drifted apart. He wanted to go out with other girls. I loved him and he fooled me into thinking he loved me, too.

Then I went through misery knowing I was carrying Bobby's child. How was I going to explain this to Bobby? After I told him, Bobby stuck by me long enough to make sure I had the operation. I went in that day by myself to do the one thing I was most against. I talked to Bobby that night, and then he took off. He stuck around long enough to make sure I got rid of the evidence, then left me on my own.

I can't explain the feelings I have inside me now. I've never thought less of myself or felt more like trash. How could I have been so naive? I loved him, but he never knew the meaning of the word. I still have nightmares and at times I hate myself. Abortion is much, much deeper than the scraping of the uterus lining. It involves one's whole being, the loss of self-respect.

A 16-year-old high school junior—
Since I started dating, I've always promised myself that I would stay a virgin until I was married. I lived up to that promise until the past year. He said he loved me and that we would get married. I really believed he loved me. After our first time, I started taking the pill to keep from getting pregnant. Two months later he dropped me for his old girlfriend (who was once pregnant by him). When I found out, I felt as if I had 200 knives go through me. I was crushed.

A 15-year-old high school sophomore—
I met this guy named Jason. He was a junior in high school and I was a sophomore. He kept pressuring me to have sex with him. He said all his friends were making fun of him and me and that all the other girls were doing it for their boyfriends. But I just couldn't give in. I was brought up in a Christian home and knew it was wrong. He would tell me he was the best that I would ever get (because of the way I looked). After a lot of this kind of treatment, I believed him. So I gave in. All I can remember is pain, and this went on for the next six months. After we had been having sex for a couple of months, he told me he would never marry me.

Before and outside of marriage, sex hurts. It destroys relationships. But purity in this area sets you up for decades of pleasure and intimacy and fulfillment and soul satisfaction in your marriage.

John and Mark were roommates in college. Although John's past had included a couple of serious mistakes, he had vowed that his next serious kiss would be with his wife. John began to date Maryanne, who lived in a dormitory nearby. Each night when he'd come home from a date, Mark would quiz him (as boys often do) about the date.

"How'd it go, man? I mean, what did you get?"

John would always reply, "Mark, I'm not like that anymore. I respect Maryanne too much to try anything."

After a year, John and Maryanne broke up. A few months later, guess who started dating Maryanne? You guessed it! Mark. They fell in love and actually got married.

John was the best man at the wedding. Afterward, John called Mark aside and whispered in his ear: "Mark, do you remember when I was dating Maryanne, how you used to ride me about not doing anything sexually with her?"

"Yeah," Mark replied. "That was so ignorant of me."

"Aren't you glad I treated her the way I did?"

Mark embraced his old roommate and fought back the tears. "You don't have any idea how deeply I appreciate you for that, John."

Ken Poure, a friend of mine from the West Coast, knows a lot about love and friendship. A few years ago his 16-year-old son came to him for advice before his first car date. Ken began to ask his son some loaded questions.

Dad: Son, are you planning on marrying this girl?

Son: Aw, nah, Dad, it's just our first date! I haven't even thought about that one.

Dad: Well, that's not unusual—only about one out of a thousand young dating relationships becomes a marriage. But let me ask you another question: Do you suppose your date will marry some guy someday?

Son: Sure, Dad. She probably will. She's a great girl.

Dad: And do you think *you* will marry a special girl someday?

Son: Oh yes, I plan on it.

Dad: Can I ask you another question?

Son: You bet.

Dad: Would you say [*he looks his son squarely in the eyes*] that your future wife is out there somewhere tonight getting herself ready to go out on a date with another boy?

Son: *[after a long pause]* Yes, sir, I think she might be going out tonight.

Dad: And this boy who is out with your future wife tonight—how do you want him to treat her?

Son: *[looking up quickly]* Dad, if he lays one hand on her, I'll kill him!

Dad: Then treat your date the same way you want that boy to treat your future wife, and you won't have any problems.

The greatest love letter ever written urges us—encourages us—commands us—to wait for sex, and then reserve it completely for our bride or groom. I believe it's the most lovingly motivated command in all of scripture! Listen to God's wisdom:

"It is God's will that you should be sanctified: that you should avoid sexual immorality; that each of you should learn to control his own body in a way that is holy and honorable, not in passionate lust like the heathen, who do not know God; and that in this matter no one should wrong his brother or take advantage of him. The Lord will punish men for all such sins, as we have already told you and warned you. For God did not call us to be impure, but to live a holy life. Therefore, he who rejects this instruction does not reject man but God, who gives you his Holy Spirit." (1 Thessalonians 4:3-8)

"Flee the evil desires of youth, and pursue righteousness, faith, love and peace, along with those who call on the Lord out of a pure heart." (2 Timothy 2:22)

"Flee from sexual immorality. All other sins a man commits are outside his body, but he who sins sexually sins against his own body." (1 Corinthians 6:18)

The rewards from heeding this advice in Scripture will never end.

TOO FAR FOR ME

At the beginning of this year, I had a friend named Rick. Rick and I would talk forever. We became so close that our feelings developed into more romance than just a friendship. We started dating, and one thing led to another. I often wondered how far was too far, but I had decided I could stop whenever I wanted to.

Whenever I was at Rick's house, we would always go to his bedroom to be alone. He had such a large family that his room was the only place we could talk. Innocently we would sit on his bed. After we started dating it was harder to just sit there with each other. Kissing came first, and we found it harder and harder to stop there. Even after we became involved in heavy petting, I still believed I could stop before we actually did it. After a few months of this, I found that I didn't want to stop. Then one night it happened —we had sex. It was worse than I could even imagine. I felt dirty and very separated from God. I hated myself for doing something I've grown up believing was so wrong. I had the guiltiest feeling I've ever had.

Rick walked me to my car and asked me what was wrong. I burst into tears. I told him that I hated it. I never wanted to do it again. Then Rick told me that he loved me, and the weirdest thing was that I couldn't tell him I loved him back. I had no feelings for him anymore. We sat in front of his house for a long time. We both cried. We knew what we did together was wrong.

I didn't see Rick for three weeks because he was out of town. During that time I prayed about it, not knowing what else to do. While we were separated, I realized what a real Christian relationship should be like, and I also realized that the relationship Rick and I had was the total opposite. I learned what was right and reassessed my morals. I asked for God's forgiveness and started my life over. I still care for Rick, but I know if we are to have a relationship it must be based on God.

Now I know that "too far" doesn't mean only inter-course, but also the stages leading up to it. Too far is when you crave the physical more than the spiritual. Too far is when sexual thoughts take over your relationship. Too far is when you don't want to stop. It can be different for different people; it can be holding hands, kissing, or hugging. For me, kissing should be the limit. I've decided not to go any further than this until I'm married. With God's help I can be pure from this day on.

KEVIN'S STORY

A SIMPLE "NO"

I found Jesus soon after I committed a sin I never should have done—I had premarital sex. The day after it hap-pened, I went to church. The preacher talked about adul-tery and premarital sex. It was then that I knew God was telling me something. Since that day I have regretted what I did, but I know Jesus has forgiven me.

Now, every day starts with a prayer and ends with one. I try to live like Jesus wants me to.

For those of you who have been faced with this decision, I encourage you to ask yourself, "Would Jesus do this?" I promise you, the answer will be NO! every time.

LINDA'S STORY

DOWN THE ROAD

As I entered eighth grade, things were going my way. I was attractive to guys, and was part of the in group at my large high school in suburban Chicago. I began to see more and more high school kids getting high. It looked like fun, and was so accepted that I began to party with them. I told myself I was just experimenting, but I did it often so I would be accepted. Once I did it, I didn't have to explain myself anymore. It was a lot easier that way, I thought. If you do it once, nine out of ten times you will do it again...and again ...and again!

That was only the beginning. I said, "I'll never do ludes." I did one and that night I did three more. I said, "I'll never do coke," but the next day I did, and then I went on and got some more. I wanted to be independent from my parents. I told them I had things under control, that I could stop whenever I wanted to. (But I always went back, and each time I got in a little deeper.)

Then one night in the ninth grade I was high on alcohol, and a guy took me to a room at a party. He undressed me and took my virginity. I felt so used and so wasted; it was so empty! I quit caring about anything. I kept getting used— and kept getting wasted.

Alcohol deadens your senses. Television makes it look okay, but inside I was dying. I lost all respect for myself. I never looked down the road at what this was doing to me. I never thought about what it would be like later in my life. I was a cheerleader, I had boyfriends, I played sports. All I looked forward to was Friday night. Little did I know that all of these highs and sex thrills were causing problems that would take years to get over.

I started to dig a hole for myself, and I couldn't get out. My grades dropped. My standards dropped. I became a do-anything girl. I hit the bottom. I got a little better, then I hit a lower bottom. Finally I ended up in a psychiatric hospital. The masks I had developed for every occasion didn't matter anymore—the fun mask I wore at parties, the flirty mask for guys, the honest mask for my parents. Now the masks were gone.

Somewhere in my childhood I was told about God's love. I began to think about all those Bible stories. Was Jesus Christ real? Did He really love me? How could He? Look at how messed up I was.

I'm not sure exactly how, but I began to accept His love. I asked Him to come into my life and forgive me. My cure didn't come from the hospital; it came from inside of me.

Back at home again, I had to give up some things and learn to say no. It started turning out right. My new friendships were built on honesty instead of alcohol. God helped me learn to respect myself. And once I realized the benefits, it became easier. God said, "I love you right where you are." With Him I felt warm inside. He said that my past doesn't affect His future for me. In His eyes I couldn't be more perfect. He totally buried my past, and it will never be dug up again. My security is in Him. The more I take my eyes off me, the happier I am.

In college now I'm different from most of my sorority sisters. They are still searching. They're getting hurt. Both of my roommates are partying constantly. At one party this year everyone except me got a room with her boyfriend. I know that the special guy I will marry someday would rather I'd wait for him to do these things. Now that I have received God's love and forgiveness, I want to be pure for my future family. I know how much they'll love me. I know how much they will need a wife and mom who is stable, secure, and dependable.

It feels so good now, not having to compromise myself. I really am happy. God's love is like that. It isn't magic, but as I remain true to Him, it feels good. It feels right.

I'm excited about life. I'm excited about my future. I'm excited about a God who brought light, love, and happiness into a life that was once so dark and dreadful that I never thought I could change. Thanks to Him, I did!

4

GREAT SEXPECTATIONS

The things that bring the greatest rewards in life when they're received also bring the greatest regrets in life when they're rejected.

Doubtless there is no greater reward imaginable than the one promised to a faithful believer in Jesus Christ: Getting to spend an entire eternity in maximum happiness—no tears, no pain, no rejection, no regrets.

God gave the vision to the apostle John in these exact words:

> *I saw the Holy City, the new Jerusalem, coming down out of heaven from God, prepared as a bride beautifully dressed for her husband. And I heard a loud voice from the throne saying, "Now the dwelling of God is with men, and he will live with them. They will be his people, and God himself will be with them and be their God. He will wipe every tear from their eyes. There will be no more death or mourning or crying or pain, for the old order of things has passed away." He who was seated on the throne said, "I am making everything new!'*
> " (Revelation 21:2-5)

The rejection of that greatest reward means spending eternity *apart* from God in a place the Bible says was constructed for Satan, his angels, and those who refuse to accept God's greatest gift of a relationship with Him through His Son.

Again God describes it:

"The sea gave up the dead that were in it, and death and Hades gave up the dead that were in them, and each person was judged according to what he had done. Then death and Hades were thrown into the lake of fire. The lake of fire is the second death. If anyone's name was not found written in the book of life, he was thrown into the lake of fire." (Revelation 20:13-15)

The second-greatest reward is the opportunity on this planet to give and receive love, to enjoy God's creation, to marvel at a baby's birth, or at a bluebird's flight, or at a Rocky Mountain sunset. It's the opportunity to be part of a team, to hug a hurting friend, to find a love letter in your mailbox, to witness to someone needing the Savior, to give a Christmas present that delights the socks off your mom, to pray with a three-year-old girl, to hear a small, tender voice calling you "Daddy," to watch a 16-year-old open his eyes after a month-long coma. This second greatest reward is what it means to be *alive*, here and now. The loss of that gift of life can come at the hands of a drug dealer, or an intoxicated driver, or a crazy world leader.

Third only to eternal life and life on earth is another gift bringing unspeakable joy: that of a man and a woman hopelessly in love and joined in holy matrimony, and who are celebrating a lifetime of intimacy sexually, emotionally, and spiritually. With this gift come a thousand other rewards of bonding.

Virginity is our gift to bring to the wedding altar. It's the tie that binds a man and woman for life. It makes a honeymoon an endless vacation in splendor, and it locks the wedding band to the ring finger like a welding torch. It frees the mind in the bedroom of sexual intimacy to behold the rare and priceless gem of oneness in purity, like the purity of a fresh blanket of newly fallen snow.

For many of us, that gem was lost in a moment of passion during a ninth-grade party, or a tenth-grade puppy love, or an eleventh-grade high. We always regret the choice, and we wonder why we fell. Eventually we ask the question, "Is a happy marriage possible for me? Will I ever find the treasure chest that houses this precious reward?"

For those who continue to reject God's plan, the answer is a sad no. No book, no drug, no party, no incredible body or beautiful face or any creative thing can ever open that treasure. God has sealed it, to eliminate man and woman's self-indulging efforts to unlock it.

But (excuse me while I climb up on a mountaintop for a moment and grab a microphone connected to 10,000-watt speakers), to the man or woman who abides by the following plan, *THE TREASURE IS YOURS!* Though you made a painful mistake (or mistakes), the key is *STILL* available to your grasp. I know many, many husbands and wives who've recognized their error and adopted the following plan, and who now enjoy marriage and sexual intimacy in terrific harmony.

From the book of the Master Surgeon, here's the plan for those who've been hurt:

SEVEN WAYS TO KEEP YOUR VIRGINITY
(OR TO GET IT BACK)

1. Your virginity is a treasure—so *guard it with your life.* Sexual purity is the greatest gift you can give your "knight in shining armor" or your "bride for a lifetime" on your wedding night. Diamonds, gold necklaces, a cruise on the Caribbean, BMWs, or any other "dream gifts" you could ever hope to give or receive don't match the gift of sexual honor and purity. No deep-sea diver has ever found a sunken treasure more delightful than the gift of honor a bride and groom are able to give each other on their wedding night.

   The hormones that hit during your teen years can sometimes be so wild and crazy that if you don't value your purity more than almost anything else you own, and guard it with an arsenal of care, it's likely to get lost in a beguiling relationship that seems so much like love for a lifetime. Even a young Sherlock Holmes in such a situation couldn't look ahead and see the ensuing heartbreak and parting that comes somewhere down the line—weeks or months or years ahead.

There is no pain like realizing you've hurt a girl you care about, when you come to your senses and look back at a broken relationship, or when you go into your wedding with no special spark left.

Guys, the leadership begins with us. That fact goes back to Adam and Eve. (You might want to check this out in the second and third chapters of Genesis.) A girl can be so vulnerable when she's crazy about you and you're doing and saying all the right things.

Often, though, after an act of passion has run its course, a guy will become distant and insensitive toward the girl. He may even put on a Mr. Macho Male swagger for his friends, and brag about his sexual conquest.

One of the biggest cover-ups in all of teenage life is an unfair double standard for guys and girls. A high school newspaper in Omaha, Nebraska described it as the crazy way that girls who have sex a lot are called "sluts," while guys who do it are called "studs." This makes it look like having sex before marriage is kind of a low-risk proposition for guys; there's glory to be gained, and it's supposedly glory without pain.

But this is all an exterior show, I assure you. Yeah, the girl often shoulders the pain with an unwanted pregnancy or an abortion, but the guy will also carry the pain for the rest of his life. Leaders are leaders. There's no way to get around it.

When your daughter is about to go out on her first date, and she stops to ask you, "Dad, by the way, how did you treat Mom when you two first dated?"—don't stutter, man! Be able to tell her truthfully that you treated her mother like a lady, enabling her later to walk down the aisle on your wedding day with her head held high and the purity of her white wedding gown fairly glowing.

Girls, it's easier than you imagine to either put the match to a guy's sexual drive, or to pour cold water on it. Realize that it takes two to dance. You can wipe out a guy with sexy perfumes like Obsession or Passion or Poison (which can do *exactly* what they say they will), and with tight pants, tight sweaters, placing your hands on his legs, kissing his ear or neck, sexy talk, etc. Don't be crazy! Girls tease guys in so many obvious ways, and guys come unglued. If you do stuff like that, don't be surprised when your treasure gets broken into and stolen. Save it all for you *husband*, and let him spend a lifetime discovering your special female beauty. If you act like a princess, you'll be treated like one. If you act like you don't care about your purity, neither will he.

Today a happy letter came to my mailbox from a bride in Texas. She said,

> "Don and I both are fortunate to have God in our hearts. Both of us understand the power of our marriage commitment to God and we both know what happened to our hearts when we said 'I do' in front of God and the audience at our wedding. Our hearts were tied together with the toughest cord around them, and God tied a knot that cannot be cut or broken. It was the most unbelievable thing in the world. When we got married, both of us by God's grace were virgins, even though we were tempted at times to give in. On our wedding night we gave each other the best present we could give each other—ourselves, pure and clean, without one tiny blemish in that special area. We could not have done it without God. We continually praise His name. It has been so worth the wait!"

God's plan is described in 1 Corinthians 7:4— "The wife's body does not belong to her alone but also to her husband. In the same way, the husband's body does not belong to him alone but also to his wife."

Get this: Some 46% of the teenage guys who've had sex with one girl have had sex with ten or more girls. And believe it or not, girls are almost as unfaithful nowadays as guys are—the current numbers are only about ten percentage points apart.

And this: The percentage of teenage boys over 15 who are having premarital sex is the same as the percentage of married men having extramarital sex behind their wife's back—the number in both cases is 60 percent. People don't change much as they leave their teen years.

2. *Write a romance novel*—on paper or in your dreams. Picture your honeymoon as a trip into Paradise, and your marriage as nothing less than the greatest story ever.

Dream big. You can't begin to outdream the reality of "love in the first degree." (As I write this chapter I'm on an airplane—which is way too slow—flying home from Florida. I miss my twentieth-anniversary bride more than any novel could describe...)

3. After you've written that romance novel in your dreams—begin to live it. *Make the novel a biography.*

My dad is wild about my mom. Every day as he goes off to work he writes her a love letter and reminds her how gorgeous she is to him. Mom dresses in lace at night. She builds Dad's dreams in the same way a skilled architect builds a hundred-story masterpiece. Dad and Mom are on a honeymoon. Funny thing is, the honeymoon started 53 years ago. Dad is 78, Mom is 39-something. Dad says Mom has the prettiest legs in the world. Who could argue with him?

For you, a lifetime of love like that begins *now*—today, tonight, Saturday night, prom night, next New Year's Eve.

My friend Bobb Biehl calls it *traction*—the "track" is the dream, and the "action" is the plan that makes the dream a reality. Look at the clothes in your closet, your perfumes, the TV shows and movies you watch, your choice of magazines and music. Get rid of everything that puts sensuous thoughts in your mind and leads you down the path of danger. When *Sassy* magazine tells you that 16-year-old sex is "normal," and *Seventeen* passionately describes French kissing fantasies, and Madonna loads up her lyrics with tempting bedroom magic—then get radical and grab the garbage disposal.

Choose the right date. Say no to the wrong kinds. Plan your dates to include fun: go-cart racing, kite-flying, steak and lobster cookouts (in groups), visiting the Porsche and BMW dealerships in town and shopping (ha!) for the $100,000 showroom model. *Exclude* plans for ever being alone in an apartment or bedroom or parked car. Exclude any testing of your self-control. *Include* a short prayer together before and after dates (really!). Remember that everyone you date is a possible lifetime mate.

4. *Live in the word of God.* Hebrews 4:12 promises that nothing else can impact your heart so deeply: "For the word of God is living and active. Sharper than any double-edged sword, it penetrates even to dividing soul and spirit, joints and marrow; it judges the thoughts and attitudes of the heart." If you want to have a problem-free dating "career," keep your heart full of God's word. Let this prayer-commitment be yours: "I have hidden your word in my heart that I might not sin against you" (Psalm 119:11).

5. *Make Christ your first love.* Jesus said, "Where your treasure is, there your heart will be also" (Matthew 6:21). If your whole sense of personal security is wrapped up in the latest love letter or Saturday night "sexpectations," you can count the days until disaster strikes. Jesus is pretty clear when He says the greatest commandment is to love the Lord your God "with *all* your heart."

Listen to the following letter which a teenage girl wrote to herself as if it were from Jesus Christ Himself. She was longing to give herself completely to someone, to have a deep soul relationship with another, to be loved thoroughly and exclusively, and the Lord responds with words about His plan for her life:

> "No, not until you are satisfied, fulfilled, and content with being loved by Me alone, with giving yourself totally and unreservedly to Me, having an

intensely personal and unique relationship with Me alone, discovering that only in Me is your satisfaction to be found—only then will you be capable of the perfect human relationship I have planned for you. You will never be united with another until you are united with Me, exclusive of anyone or anything else, exclusive of any other desires or longings. I want you to stop planning, to stop wishing, and allow Me to give you the most thrilling plan there is—one that you cannot imagine. I want you to have the best. Please allow Me to give it to you. Just watch Me, expecting the satisfaction that I am to you. Keep listening and learning the things I tell you.

"Just wait—that's all. Don't be anxious. Don't look at the things you want. Don't look away from Me, or you'll miss what I want to show you. And then, when you're ready, I'll surprise you with a love far more wonderful than any you could ever dream of.

"You see, until you are ready (I am working even at this moment to have you both ready at the same time), until you are both satisfied exclusively with Me and the life I have prepared for you, you will not be able to experience the love that exemplifies your relationship with Me. And, dear one, I want you to have the most wonderful love! I want you to see in the flesh a picture of your relationship with Me, and to enjoy materially and concretely the everlasting union of beauty, perfection, and love that I offer you with Myself.

"Know that I love you utterly. I am God Almighty. Believe it. Believe Me, and be satisfied."

6. **Stop playing games.** God tells us to "throw off everything that hinders and the sin that so easily entangles" (Hebrews 12:1). He means to take that old line about everything except "all the way" being A-OK, and send it back to the editor of *Sassy*. Petting leads to intercourse—always has, always will. Heavy kissing leads to petting—always has, always will.

I learned to drive with a manual four-speed transmission. You had to shift gears purposefully. My daughter drives an "automatic." The gears shift without any effort at all. First gear wraps to about 20 MPH, then automatically kicks into second. Second gear shoots her up to about 35 MPH, then third kicks in. Sex is an automatic transmission. Don't kid yourself for a second. Nearly every pregnant 16-year-old was "only petting" just a few months before. Every kid with AIDS and syphilis was "only fooling around a little" just a while back.

A 17-year-old unmarried mother came to a friend of mine a few years ago, seeking advice. She was hurting badly, her tears had been many, and she couldn't "go it alone." She had failed to "flee the temptation." During her junior year in high school she met a guy who was everything a girl could ask for. He was the most popular guy in school, he was cute, and he was a talented athlete. But his reputation with girls was bad. He prided himself in "always getting what he wanted" on a date. She was attracted to him, but turned off by his reputation.

Then she got a phone call. He asked her to a movie. A little red flag went up in her mind. Her emotions were calm; she had about ten seconds to say no and "flee" the situation. But she rationalized: *There will be lots of people there... Maybe I can help him.* "Okay," she said, "I'll go."

He picked her up as planned. She stayed on her side of the seat. As they passed the theater, he said, "I've already seen that show, and it's boring. Let's go to the beach. Lots of kids are down there, and we can play some volleyball and stuff." The second red flag went up in her mind. She again felt in control, and rationalized that with all the kids around, there would be no problems. She said, "Let's go."

When they got to the beach, no one was there. "Wow," he said, "the party must have moved. Let's just sit here and talk a little while." The third red flag went up. The pressure was growing, she had less time to make decisions, and she found it harder and harder to say no. She agreed to stay.

After thirty minutes of chatter, he moved over to her side of the seat. He calmly put his arm around her shoulders and began to "make his moves" to arouse her emotions. The fourth red flag in her mind went up, and it was big and easy to see.

The flags kept flying, and she kept giving in. Nine months later she gave birth to an unwanted, fatherless baby.

7. *If you've failed, find forgiveness in Christ.* Forgiveness is like taking a hundred-pound weight off your back and running a hundred-yard-dash. Nothing restores and preserves your purity like a true embracing of Christ's work on the cross.

When it comes to past sexual sin, there are two kinds of memories. One type comes to you like a rainstorm on a dark, scary night. The other comes like golden sunlight on a summer day. Both are dangerous. The first is depressing, de-motivating. The second tempts further sin. The stormy night version is that nagging guilt problem. You made a sexual mistake, you regret it, you're sincerely sorry you were ever there in the first place. The sunny day version is a past sexual sin that makes you smile as you relive the conquest (for guys) or the intimacy of the relationship (for girls). Both memories are from the enemy, and need to be treated with all-out war. *God forgets sin once it's been properly dealt with—and so should we!* Satan's favorite weapon is to drag up the old bones and get you to stumble all over again, as the memory comes to life.

How about a good funeral today? *Bury* those past mistakes, and stomp the dirt on top. Man, that feels great!

FREE TO BE ME

I have not felt so free in such a long time! The last couple of years in my life have really been the hardest and most painful times I can remember.

It started when I dated this guy at my school. We went out for almost a year and I really thought I loved him. In the beginning, everything was great. I was like every girl in this world, wanting a guy to like me and care about me, and my boyfriend did. I knew he wasn't a Christian and he drank, but I was all set to change him and his life.

Further into our relationship I spent all my time thinking about him. I rebelled against my parents and their rules constantly. I lost a lot of friends and became dependent on my boyfriend. Our relationship became heavily centered around making out, and I started to feel like he just used me a lot of the time. He knew I wouldn't have sex with him because I was saving that for marriage, but the pressures started to build. Sometimes we would be together after he had been drinking. He would get mad at the littlest things and yell and sometimes hit me. It was like a crazy world, but I just stayed there. I would cry a lot, and I was really scared of making him angry; but if he was, I always tried to apologize so I wouldn't lose him. He was my security.

The first time he cheated on me, I can't even describe the pain I felt. I thought he loved me and cared about me. All of his promises turned into lies, and it hurt so bad. But I always went back.

The same kind of relationship continued, except the pressure got worse and fear was always there. I felt like I was on a roller coaster with my emotions or trapped in a lion's cage. Finally he broke up with me, and that was about all I could handle. I cried day and night, and stopped eating. He constantly harassed me about his other girls and cut me down, but he still said he loved me. I finally got to the breaking point where I couldn't take one more thing. I hated everyone around me, and all I thought about was the hurt I felt. I still wanted him back even though a part of me hated him. I tried to commit suicide, but luckily I didn't succeed.

A day later I gave all the shattered pieces of my life to God. He picked me up and helped me get back on my feet. It wasn't easy, and I had a lot of hurt for a long time. It took forever for my feelings to mend and my hurt to go away, but God was there the entire time.

Now, about a year later, I have learned to bury the past and put it all behind me. The biggest obstacle I had was forgiving myself for all the things I had done. God forgave me and loves me, and He has an awesome life planned for me. So I buried the past and am looking forward to God's plan. When you see me today you see a new person in Christ. I smile a lot and feel good about myself again. As it says in 2 Corinthians 5:17,

> *"If anyone is in Christ, he is a new creature; the old things are passed away; behold, new things have come."*

THE CLASSIC

Look at a young woman's face—at the tear of brokenness falling from her eye, the look of astonishment on her brow, the glow of amazement on her lips. Then behold the man beside her—the compassion radiating from his rugged face, the tenderness in the touch of his fingertips.

The scene is my favorite moment in Scripture. The story is told in John 8, by the disciple who knew Jesus' heart the best.

The situation was probably a scam—most likely a setup to embarrass the woman and put the Messiah in a trap: The religious leaders of the day had caught the woman in the act of adultery. As was the custom, they brought her to a rocky area outside of town where they would gather around her and throw rocks at her until they knocked her to the ground, then continue the barrage until the victim's lips were still and her breathing ceased.

The Rock was also there...not to be hurled in judgment, but to make a point—perhaps to start an earthquake. Someone got up enough nerve to consult Jesus. The others jeered as the pious Pharisee posed the question designed to entrap this noted Teacher: "Sir, the Law says to stone her, but you speak of forgiveness. What do you say now?"

Jesus simply wrote in the sand. Perhaps He wrote to take the focus and embarrassment away from the woman. Perhaps He simply wrote their secret sins at the feet of each of the self-appointed judges—a secret girlfriend here, a dishonest deal there. Whatever He wrote, He straightened up after a while and said, "Let him among you who is without sin cast the first stone."

Thud, thud, thud. The rocks fell loosely from their hands as His truth hit rock bottom in each of their hearts. One by one they left the scene of the would-be murder. Soon everyone was gone except one scared girl—and the one reliable God, who became a Man to bring you and me an eternal message.

He broke the silence: "Woman, where are your accusers?"

She stammered in amazement, "There are none, Lord. They're all gone."

Then the Lord spoke the message that changed my cob-webbed heart, and can change yours as well: "Then neither do I condemn you. Go, sin no more." He was saying, "Go, turn from your past, and follow Me closely. I'll restore to you everything you've lost, and more!"

Dignity restored, forgiveness accomplished, and salvation established, she walked away from the Savior a new girl.

Now look at His face again. Call Him "Friend" when you talk to Him.

A 16-year-old girl told me recently that her boyfriend took her virginity and then iced the cake by telling her that only virgins get good husbands. Nothing could be further from the truth!

Yes, virginity is best. But forgiveness with total repentance is also best. The sinner who keeps on playing with fire is headed for a life of disaster. But the guy or girl who's stained—like me —still has everything good in life and family to look forward to, because Christ forgives...*everything*.

A friend of mine drove a Corvette off the showroom floor. My kids and I are putting a hand-polished new coat of paint on our newly restored '66 Mustang convertible. It's a work of art as we sand it down and polish it together.

I'll never have a Corvette. Sure, it would be so sweet to drive one off the showroom floor some day. But that's not my lot in life.

You may be a Corvette. If so, I'm proud of you. I appreciate you. You're a virgin and you have every right to feel great about your purity. Don't give it up until you say "I do." Give that Corvette as a wedding gift.

Or maybe you're more like a '66 Mustang Classic. You've been driven before—but Christ has restored you. New paint, new engine, new interior, new roof, fresh from top to bottom.

We drive our Mustang Classic carefully. If you will also, you'll have the joy of intimacy with God and intimacy in your marriage.

5

THE STING OF REJECTION

The sting of rejection first hit the bull's-eye in my heart in fifth grade. Of all the painful moments in my life, that one probably remains at the top of the list. I was standing outside my next-door neighbor's house on a Saturday afternoon. Four of our neighborhood friends (the guys I thought the most of) were playing inside. I could see through the window that they were watching a football game on TV, drinking Cokes and having a blast. I turned the doorknob to go in and was surprised to find it locked. I knocked and said something like, "Hey, in there. Open up, somebody."

A voice from inside replied, "Can't you see? No one is home."

I'm a little slow sometimes, and it took me a while to put two and two together. "Nobody's home?" I asked, "How can nobody be home when there are five people in there?"

"Get a hint, man. Buzz off."

I got the hint. My heart broke in half. I was unwanted. These guys were my friends. All I had left was my room...a place for solitude and self-pity.

Kids can be cruel in the growing-up years.

My first girlfriend in junior high dropped me for one of my "buddies." Asking a girl to dance often brought me rejection and disappointment. In the school cafeteria, I often ate alone. I watched as classmates would look for a seat (with two obvious openings on either side of me) and then reject my spot for another. The feelings sent knives into my stomach.

Choosing up sides for a backyard football or baseball game was something I dreaded. To a young boy, getting picked last is the ultimate pie in the face. Standing there alone—trying to make myself look athletic and attractive so one of the two captains would pick me—was such a slam to my pride. Wow! It's pitiful, looking back.

My first reaction to the war of rejection was simple hurt and loneliness. Then I began working to gain acceptance by being a chameleon...changing my personality to fit each situation, so I wouldn't offend anyone and get rejected. It drove me crazy! I ended up with no personality of my own, no security in myself. I would actually change masks in the middle of a conversation when I saw that one mask wasn't working. The mask stage was worse than the lonely stage—by far.

At age 17, when I was attending summer camp, I stumbled into a small group of counselors late one night who were praying under a giant elm tree near the cabins. They asked me to join them. I was flattered to be asked, so I stayed.

They asked me if I had ever asked Jesus into my heart as my Lord, Savior, and Friend. I didn't understand what they meant, so they went on to explain that He had come to the earth as God's Son, to die for my sins (I knew I needed that), and that if I believed in Him for who He was, and asked Him to come into my life, and made a commitment to live for Him, then according to His word He would live in my heart forever.

That moment was so incredibly real to me. I prayed a very sincere prayer to accept His Spirit into my heart, and I raised my head knowing my life was different. I had a simple peace in my heart, knowing that Someone cared.

The next year in high school I knew who I was. I didn't wear a giant cross or anything, but for the first time in my life I had something to stand on. I devoured the New Testament like it was chocolate candy. I couldn't get enough of it. It became my road map for decisions. It gave me security. I threw away the masks, and though I still struggled with rejection at times, life was drastically different. I was shocked when I was elected captain of the football team, and almost fainted when my name was read aloud for other honors. I knew there must be a mistake, or that someone was pulling my leg.

For two tough years in college, those terrible rejection fears returned. In my plain blue jeans and cowboy boots, and with my sub-average athletic talent, I walked onto a slick college campus of sporty cars and designer clothes and blue-chip athletes. I struggled hard, but the Lord stuck with me and kept me on my feet. The biggest rejection of all came shortly after graduation when my wife walked away with my best friend. I was crushed, but never lost hope. I've never been closer to God than I was during those tearful days and nights.

To this day I have a soft spot for hurting kids. I'm always ready for a letter or phone call or conversation with a teenager or little kid who is like I was. Even though it's been decades since junior high, I'm always touched with gratitude when someone chooses to sit by me at a table somewhere. I still can't get over it. When I sing a neat hymn at church, I often get teary-eyed to think about that Man who died for me. When my wife, Debbie-Jo, and our kids snuggle up beside me on the living room couch, no one knows how incredibly special I feel to be loved like that.

You know what? If I had it all to do over again, I wouldn't change my past! Being the little loser taught me to care. My kids have suffered from rejection at times during junior high and high school. It's so easy to drop everything and be there for them.

When Jamie, my oldest daughter, was seven and a half, her heart was firmly encamped in a rigorous gymnastics school. The training was hard, but she felt the rewards were worth it. We would travel to gymnastic meets throughout the winter and fill our lives with the cheers and tears of the competitive gymnastics world.

One evening Jamie came home from practice. A quick glance at her face told me that this evening was not like the rest. She had just been cut from the A team and placed on the B team.

As tears streamed down her face and disappointment broke her heart, I pulled her into my lap and we rocked in the rocking chair as only daddies and little girls can do. I began to console her by telling her the many stories of when I had been cut from an A to the B team, and worse. I looked her in the eyes, brushed away her tears, and said, "Jamie, God doesn't care what team you're on. He only cares about your heart—and little princess, you have the biggest heart of anyone I know."

After about twenty-five minutes she seemed to be okay. She bounced out of my arms and was on her way back to her happy little carefree world. That night, as I tucked Jamie into bed, we prayed together and memorized our nightly Bible verse, and I walked quietly toward the door. Just as I got to the doorway, I heard her little voice penetrate the darkness. "Daddy, thanks for tying my heart back together tonight."

I stood there in amazement. I walked over to her bed, held my face next to her soft, little-girl cheek, and whispered into her ear, "What did you say, Peanut?"

"I just said thank you for tying my heart back together tonight."

I stammered for words. "What did you mean by that, Jamie?"

She whispered softly, "Well, tonight, when I came in from gymnastics, my heart was broken, but you tied it back together again."

Everyone, I've found, gets rejected from time to time. Kids are so hard on other kids. Rejection is common ground for us all. Being a veteran with lots of battle ribbons and scars from that war, I think I'm qualified to offer you some sound counsel.

First, *you're not alone.* Don't let yourself be fooled into thinking you're the only one who gets rejected.

Second, *it will end,* and you will be a more sensitive, caring, loving person when it does.

Third, *be yourself.* Don't change who God made you to be for anyone. When some kind of a mask looks tempting, don't buy it. You were made to know God and follow Christ with your life. Any substitute face will be a letdown to you, to your family, and to everyone who knows you.

Fourth, *follow Christ!* In Isaiah 53 we read that Jesus had no great outward appearance, and yet He was definitely the most intimately attractive man who ever lived. Take note of this! As you give more and more of your heart to Him, the Holy Spirit's work in your life makes you more like Christ. That's why my senior year in high school was so different. By God's grace, people saw Christ in me. That's why my wife of 18 years gets more attractive to me every year of her life! As she grows in Christ, I see more and more of Him in her.

At our camp we have about six thousand kids from around the world. Many of them are rock-solid teenagers. They are honestly the most intimately attractive teenagers I've ever known. Some are very poor, some very rich; some are All-Americans, some can't make all-backyard! Some are Miss Americas. Some are quite plain (like me). But the ones everyone likes the most are those who are moving along in this amazing process of getting transformed into the image of their Savior.

If you're not already, I urge you to get on board and ride this train. Its destination is the station with no regrets.

CHRISTINA'S STORY

"CHRISTINKA"

Only a few days ago I realized rejection is okay. It's necessary. It's important. It's a normal part of life. And I faced a bunch of it growing up. Rejection was a regular part of my life, and still is.

The pain that so often accompanied rejection at one time seemed unbearable. My feet turn slightly inward whenever I walk. I would never admit that, until I saw a wonderful man admit to a crowd of people that he, too, was "pigeon-toed." I realized that being pigeon-toed did not automatically condemn me to lifelong failure.

Kids are smart. They can make you hurt worse than taking a gunshot wound from point-blank range. I was in second grade when my classmates discovered I was pigeon-toed.

"Look! She walks like a bird! Ha!"

"Bird nerd! Bird nerd!"

Those names hurt so much. I spent most of my days that year concentrating on the position of my feet as I sat and walked from place to place. Once I spent an entire summer practicing straight-walking every day. I walked along the white and yellow lines painted on the street, along the curb, and up and down the cracks in the sidewalk. What a waste of a summer; I'm still pigeon-toed today.

I think children begin to develop a mean streak as they enter the second grade. They also gave me another name that year. And although no one has called me that since, the memory still hurts sometimes.

"Run! Here comes 'Christinka'!"

"Hey, 'Christinka,' what's your problem?"

When we lined up in the hall to go to the next class, the person in front of me would say, "Ooh! It's Christinka," then run to the back of the line. No matter where I originally stood in line, I'd always end up at the front.

"What's your problem, Christinka?" they'd ask. I didn't know what my problem was. I sure dedicated an incredible amount of time attempting to figure it out, though. I knew I didn't fit in. No one wanted to sit by me at lunch. No one invited me to birthday parties or sleep-overs. No one ever wanted to play with me at recess. What *was* my problem?

Was it my clothes? I didn't wear the latest styles that most of the kids sported. I was not involved with the Bluebirds, the Brownies, the Girl Scouts. Was it my hair? *That's it!* I thought. *It must be my hair.* It was too long, and so blonde it looked white. Most of the kids had darker hair. I began to wish mine was dark, too, after a few children said "Hey, Casper—*Boo!*" Once I took a black marker and colored my eyebrows. My sister told me they were too light, and no one could see them. Well, you could see them after that; they stayed dark for weeks.

I used to want so badly for someone to really be my friend. That desire usually meant I was in for big trouble. Once, while I was at nursery school, Raza, the owner's niece, asked me to seesaw with her.

"Okay," I said. *Wow!* I thought. *She wants to play with me.* Cautiously approaching the rocker-bottomed seesaw, I waited for her to sit first, then took a seat at the opposite side. We began slowly, but soon she began to greatly increase the height of our journey. Up and down, up and down, back and forth. I began to get a sick feeling.

"Can I please get off now?" I asked. She didn't respond.

"I want to get off," I told her. She rocked even harder.

"I want to stop! Please?" Even faster we progressed.

"I'm going to—"

BAM! CRASH! It ended. She jumped off as I was on an upward journey. Demolished beneath the metal bar of the cast-iron seesaw was my bloody face. It hurts just to remember the pain I felt upon impact.

I was shivering with fear. No one came to help. I didn't make a sound; I don't think I could have.

Raza stood there laughing as I looked at her with fear and panic in my eyes. She found amusement in my severe pain. Her cruel look was as frightening as the bland taste of blood oozing slowly but surely down the base of my swollen throat. Fear penetrated my body, as blood seeped down my cheeks, plinked off the back of my neck, and splashed to the ground.

When Mrs. Doltz (the owner of the nursery school) came on the scene, along with Raza's mother, Raza acted completely innocent. She had made it clear to me beyond any doubt that she had jumped on purpose. Her entire reason for inviting me to join her was to watch me fly. However, as she stood there being questioned about what had happened, my deathlike paleness caused no shame or remorse to cloud her conscience. She denied everything. Later, I was taken to the hospital for examination. I had to wear the stitches for two weeks, the cast for three months, and the scars for the rest of my life.

How many times have *you* been scarred by rejection? I'm not just talking about the external scars; I'm talking about the internal ones. What about the scars that don't quit hurting when the stitches come out?

I asked Jesus Christ to come live in my heart as my personal Lord and Savior when I was 15 years old, after Todd, a great friend, shared with me how to obtain an incredible personal relationship with the one and only God. Todd told me how beginning a personal relationship with Jesus had filled the void in his life. And he told me it could fill my void, too. As Todd and I prayed together that night, I had no idea what was to come.

The next few years were full of questions, temptations, and trials. They were also full of good Christian friends, something I'd never known before. They were full of heavenly love that I had never been able to feel. These were years filled with incredible growth, too. And those special friends, that unfailing love, and that constant growth that a true personal relationship with Jesus Christ brings about have shown me why God allows rejection in our lives. Here's the reason:

R *evealing*
E *verlasting*
J *esus faced*
E *levates*
C *ures*
T *enderizes*
I *nsures growth*
O *pens doors*
N *eeded*

Rejection is *revealing.* It allows you to look at yourself as others sometimes see you. At times is has helped me work on my faults. At other times it has forced me to rely on God and the knowledge that I'm perfect now in His eyes.

Rejection is *everlasting.* It continues. It doesn't stop coming as you grow older. I think it's something we all face in some way from the day we are born until the day we die.

Rejection is something *Jesus* faced. His best friends turned their backs on Him as He died for them. Jesus set the example to show me how I should face rejection.

Rejection *elevates* your relationship with Christ and affects your personality and your decisions. It's like the time I colored my eyebrows. I did it so people would better accept me. But our decisions should be based on whether or not *God* would accept them. Had God wanted me to have dark hair, He would have created me with dark hair. Our friends, our classmates, and our fellow workers will not decide where we will make our final move for eternity; God will.

Rejection *cures* as it appears to hurt. No doubt about it— whenever someone tells you to get lost because you're ugly, it hurts. But many times you can look back on it, and smile. A friend of mine once told me how his "friends" would ridicule him and run away when he approached them. "It was pitiful," he laughed. "They were mean; they were cruel."

He laughed. But my first reaction was to cry. *Here is one of the nicest people I know, and people were cruel to him as he grew up. Why does he laugh? It's not funny! It's sad!*

Or is it? I actually don't know why he laughed. But today I laughed at Christinka for the first time. Why? I laughed because I'm so happy now. I'm learning and growing, and my friends are the best in the world. And those kids I grew up with are recovering from alcoholism, abortion scars, and drug defects. Some of them are not yet on the road to recovery; they are still wandering around lost. Rejection helped make my friend who he is today, and it has helped make me who I am today. And today's rejection will become part of who you are tomorrow.

Rejection *tenderizes.* I'm the last person to go around spitting out criticism. The rejection that I've felt in the past has allowed me to befriend others with compassion and forgiveness.

Rejection *insures growth.* All the thought and emotion we pour into what others think about us allows us to grow intellectually, emotionally, and spiritually.

Rejection *opens doors* in your heart. It's wonderful to feel so compassionately for others' hurts. I don't think there's anything negative about that quality in my character.

Rejection is *needed!* It is! I wouldn't be who I am today if I hadn't busted my face on the seesaw so many years ago.

MIKE'S STORY

REAL FRIENDS

It was my high school freshman year, and exams were all over with. We were biking home due to the fact that we couldn't drive. It was Matt, Peter, and me. As we were nearing Matt's house, Matt and Peter said, "Goodbye, Mike," as if they didn't want me there. It was hard to take, because I wanted so badly to be with them. Who knows what they were going to do? I just wanted to be friends.

I stood there for a while and watched them bike off, laughing. It wasn't that bad at first, because I knew three was a crowd. So I started biking home. All of a sudden I started crying like I'd never cried before. The whole way home I had trouble seeing because tears were flooding my eyes. I arrived home wiping the tears away so Mom wouldn't see. But I couldn't hold it, and I told her what happened. I said I wanted to leave the school I attended and go to a new one.

That very day I applied at a new school and was accepted the next day—which is hard to believe because of the difficulty of getting into the school. And boy, was my life changed there!

I share this with you for two reasons. First, I want to urge you to know your friends. All my friends did was use me. Choose your friends wisely!

Second, I want to say it wasn't *me* that told me to go home. It wasn't *me* that got me accepted to a new school. It was God. Without that specific incident—no joke!—my whole future could have been ruined. God saved me.

From here on, I've learned who are my right friends and who are my wrong ones. But wherever I am, I always have a Best Friend—and He's in Heaven.

BETH'S STORY

RISKY BUSINESS

I got a letter from one of my best friends, Nicole. She had a big crush on her brother's best friend, Nick, who was three years older than she. She had liked him for a long time. She was babysitting his little brother a lot, and Nick would use her. Only she thought he loved her. Another girl and I (the three of us are really close) were trying to tell Nicole how wrong it was. This was my first experience where it wasn't somebody I had just heard about; I knew this girl! And I was so afraid for her.

Nicole had recently lost her father. Her brother, age 16, had recently turned to alcohol. (Fortunately, that was only temporary.) Now she had turned to Nick. I knew I wasn't being a true friend if I didn't remind her what Jesus would think. But I was scared. I knew I was risking a lot. She could either be thankful that I reminded her, and try to turn herself around, or she could get mad—and I would lose her friendship. But I had to take that risk. I couldn't be selfish about a friendship.

I confronted Nicole face to face. As a friend, I told her how she was hurting herself. She was mad, not only about what I said, but also that I didn't trust her. But when I later saw her, the other friend and I talked to her, and I think she came to the realization of how wrong she and Nick were. Now she hates him and feels so dirty for what she did. But she also understands she is forgiven by Christ, and that He's turned her heart inside out and made it clean again.

Sometimes friendship is risky business. But knowing that Jesus risked everything to come to earth and die on a wooden cross makes it easy to take that risk for someone you call a friend.

Although I'm not always the most loyal Christian, it's so refreshing and wonderful to know God loves me like that, and gave all He had for me! It's almost like hearing about Jesus for the first time.

6

SWEET TARTS

Jumbo shrimp, horse fly, pretty ugly, light weight, sweet tart, love's over—*oxymorons* is what they're called: opposites or contradictions that are put together in pairs. It's fun to make up new ones and laugh at how silly they sound.

Life is like an oxymoron. Sugar and lemon together make make something great. (I like lemonade). And so do the nice things and the hard things in life.

Bees sting, and bees make honey. Being sick makes me appreciate being well. Being sad makes me appreciate happiness. Rain makes the next sunny day seem more beautiful. Losing a football game always made victory smell sweeter.

Have you tasted tragedy? So have many friends of mine, and they're learning the good that can come from it.

SANDI'S STORY

DOUBLE DEATH!

At age 14 something happened in my life that will forever shape my attitude toward the deadliest drug ever known —alcohol. I will never forget when Mom told me Daddy was very sick. My dad was a hopeless alcoholic.

Alcohol made my parents unhappy. Marriage counseling didn't help. Daddy just could not control his drinking. He finally moved out when my parents couldn't solve their problems, and things began to go downhill rapidly for him.

My daddy had gone to Princeton and Harvard, but he couldn't even get a job because of the effect alcohol had on his life. He began to hallucinate, and told weird stories. My brother, David, had just gotten his driver's license, and he was always out with his friends, so I would go over and cook for Daddy and try to console him.

Soon he began to lose his appetite. All he did was drink. His skin began to turn yellow, and we knew he was dying. We tried to hospitalize him but he refused. Mom worked hard to prepare us for what she thought was inevitable.

Just when my parents were about to get a divorce, Daddy passed out and went into a coma from which he never recovered. During those days I leaned on David more than I did my own Mom. Even though it had been cool not to like your brother at times, David and I became close through the tragedy of losing Dad. We spent many evenings sorting everything out together. My brother told me he was afraid that he, too, was an alcoholic. Even though he was just 18, he knew he had to be really careful.

Two months later, during spring break, I was in Galveston, Texas, and David was in Houston. He was supposed to come down to see me one evening. I called him and called him, but no one answered the phone. I suspected that something had gone wrong.

The next morning I found out David had been killed. Later I learned from two of David's friends that he had gone to a party and met up with a guy with a new Camaro. The guy was drunk, but he wanted to show David how fast the Camaro would run. While they were going around a curve, the car went off the road and crashed into a guardrail that split the car in half. David was killed instantly.

I couldn't believe what had happened. I was just sort of numb. Then I cried unceasingly. I went home, and learned that mom was due to arrive at the airport, and didn't know what had happened. I went with friends to the airport to tell her of David's death. It was awful.

I prayed a lot, but I never got mad at God or told Him it was His fault. God has always provided me with good friends. And through it all, I learned the value of prayer a lot more. I'll never take prayer for granted again.

The pain is probably greater now than ever. The Lord is really my best friend. He's been through it all with me. Through it all I had hope. No matter how much I give Him, no matter how bad, He handles it. If He could love me when I was at my worst, then I know He love me now.

I don't know why people can't see how bad alcohol is. It is very deceiving. It hurts! It kills.

I'm a different person now. The tragedy in my life taught me to never give up hope. And it forced me to love my mom the way I should have loved her all along.

A BETTER PLACE FOR MOM

Four months ago my mom passed away. What an awesome lady she was! When Mom got sick, the thing she hated most was not being able to serve us.

Mom had bone cancer. I was at baseball practice talking to a girl whose mom had died of cancer when I found out Mom needed to have some tests. I was worried that her tests would be positive. Our family is the type that never gives up, so we all made a pact. We never gave up faith; we never turned bitter.

It was God's will for her to leave us now. I'm thankful for the time we had together. I learned so much from her.

Mom painted a lot. She loved nature and had such a knowledge of God. Mom was such a witness! She never quit. I'm so glad I had a mom who had faith like that to influence my walk with God.

In the district finals in cross country, shortly before Mom died, I told her I would bring her a medal. Mom was in surgery on the day of the big meet. I'm not a great runner, but I led the pack the first two miles and ended up with the medal I prayed for. Mom was so happy.

Thirty minutes after she died, my brother, my dad, and I got into a huddle. Dad said, "No more pain. Now she's in heaven, rejoicing."

God has shown us a giant love during this time. It's still hard. To this day I expect to get letters from her when I'm away, but I know I won't. I'm so glad I have Jesus in my heart. What would I do if I didn't?

Mom had told me that I would have to be the spiritual leader after she left. Now, when things are hard, I don't give up. I never surrender, because Mom didn't. Jesus didn't, and that knowledge gives me strength.

I made a necklace to remind me of Mom. It has my silver cross with silver tennis shoes and my Mom's ring. Every time I look in the mirror it reminds me of my athletic training, Mom, and God.

When someone close to them dies, a lot of kids ask, "Why?" But I say, "Don't be bitter, because God has a reason." God doesn't take you home until it's your time.

Don't blame yourself when someone dies in your family. That person knows you care.

Our God is an awesome God. He'll love you till death. The best thing to do is to lead those you love to Christ, because you never know when you might lose a loved one. Mom taught me to witness whenever I had the opportunity. Now I know why.

7

THE LAST WORD
IS GOOD

Take a look in the Old Testament at the man named Joseph. He was neglected, abused, ridiculed, and kicked out by his family. His brothers mistreated him, his peers rejected him, his employer falsely accused him, and a powerful woman tried to seduce him. A king finally realized his potential and sat Joseph on his throne.

Before long, Joseph found the family who had rebuked him sitting at his feet begging for food. Joseph was a godly man with the same godly attitude as many of the kids whose stories you're reading in this book. He treated his family with total respect. He never lost sight of the sovereignty of God. Joseph never stopped believing there was a diamond in the old black coal that buried him. Later he was able to tell his brothers, "You meant it for evil, yet God used it for good."

God always gets in the last word, and that word is a good word.

KRISTY'S STORY

LEARNING TO LOVE AGAIN

It all started three years ago when my sister moved out to go to college. My dad works out of town, so he's not home very often to see what's going on. I have a little brother who is three years younger than I am. When my sister moved out, it was just my mom and brother and me most of the time.

My brother, the youngest child and only boy, is a slow learner, so my mom has always shown favoritism toward him. When my dad and sister were around, I always had them to lean on, and my life was great. I was popular, made great grades, and was very athletic. After my sister moved out, things changed. For some reason I lost most of my friends, and my grades went down, but mostly I had no one to lean on because my mom acted like she didn't care. Every time something went wrong at home, I got the blame. She didn't beat me; she would just yell.

After I found God, things changed again. I had Someone to lean on, and Someone to talk to who would listen. My grades picked back up a little. I got a whole new set of Christian friends who loved me for who I am, and now I get along better with my mom.

I wrote to my sister the other day and told her all this stuff about God and how we have Him, and we have each other. I also said we should forgive Mom because she isn't perfect and some day she will see what she has missed out on. But I know now that Mom is the only mother I have, and I can't trade her in for a new one; even if I could, I wouldn't. Because I see she is so wonderful and I love her very much.

COREY'S STORY

A SISTER TO LOVE AGAIN

My sister was an okay student in high school. She was popular, too. But way back in her early years in high school she started drinking and going into a place in town where all the bands hung out and where all the bars were. She didn't graduate because her math teacher didn't like her and wouldn't give her the two points she needed to pass the class. So when she got out of school she started partying a lot. She started to drink a lot too, and to hang out with all the druggies.

Some nights my sister would dress up funky. Sometimes she wouldn't come home. This worried my parents to death. Even on the nights when she did come home, she was always drunk and late. My parents said she couldn't go out anymore. So she would climb out her window. When she got home my parents would yell at her. I loved my sister, so I got mad at my parents. Then I realized my parents were right, and I got mad at my sister. I was about nine or ten during all this.

Then Mom got my sister into a treatment center. When she got out, we thought she was well. But she wasn't. She had a slip. She got her own apartment and got drunk one night. She saw some people who had some beer, and invited them in for a party. They turned out to be skinheads. They trashed her place, burned her cat's whiskers off, stole stuff, and tried to cut my sister. She got scared and ran. Then she went into treatment for the second time.

Later she had another slip, and went into treatment again at a different place. She was straight for about six months. Then, while our family was on vacation, she started having pain. She was pregnant. That was a surprise, but as it turns out this was for the best. She couldn't drink because that would have hurt the baby. So for another six months she was straight. During this period she started to look for God and found Him. He helped her through the delivery. Now she goes to church and listens to Christian music. She got me started. I love her a lot. She's been straight for about a year now. God gave us a miracle and held our family together.

I LOVE YOU, DAD

Dad is the man who has loved me through the best and worst times, a man who has sacrificed and devoted his life to his family. But for some reason I just didn't like Dad very much. He and I have very different personalities and I found it hard to relate to him. It's amazing how messed up my heart became because I was out of fellowship with my dad.

I will never forget that bright June afternoon when I was challenged by a godly counselor at summer camp to make an effort to develop my relationship with Dad. Through his guidance I wrote out an action plan that would help me learn to love Dad whether or not I understood him. Somehow, when you learn to love someone for exactly who he is (not just what he's given you), it's much easier to relate to that person!

I went home from camp and wasn't exactly sure the action plan was worth the time (yes, it took some), effort (plenty of that, too), and love (the most necessary ingredient) that it required. However, as I am slowly learning, God is the Provider of that time, effort, and love. I want this message to come through loud and clear: I could not have worked through this action plan on my own. God was the doer of the whole thing. He worked through me to set the plan into action.

Here's what I decided to do for my dad:

1. Once a week, ask Dad to wake up early with me so we can pray together for our family.
2. Help Dad paint the house.
3. Once a week, make him a nutritious snack to take to the office.

4. Stock his refrigerator at his office with nutritious munchies once every two weeks.
5. Serve him breakfast in bed once every two weeks.
6. Once a month, offer to go up to his office with him to help him get caught up on any work, clean for him, etc.
7. Ask him to spend time with me going over college material.
8. Tell him "I love you" every day.
9. Give him specific compliments every day.
10. Hug him every day.
11. Offer to do the grocery shopping once every two weeks.
12. Take out the trash (collect, bag it, etc.) twice a week.
13. Don't ask for money for "fun" things.
14. Make time to talk to him every day.
15. Ask him to have Bible study or devotions with me once a week.
16. Send him a note with just the words, "I love you!—Brooke."
17. Give him a blown-up picture of myself with a big sign that says, "I love you, Daddy."
18. Send him a letter with a friendship bracelet enclosed.
19. Make him a painted T-shirt.
20. Fix and serve him dinner with all his favorite foods.
21. Make him a date to play miniature golf together.
22. Make a list of all the qualities I admire in him and want to have.
23. Take over the yard work (mow, rake, trim, etc.).
24. Help him plan a special surprise for Mom.
25. Write him a poem.
26. Buy a watermelon, take Dad to the park, and have a watermelon-eating and seed-spitting contest.
27. "Kidnap" him from his office one day during lunch, and take him on a picnic.

28. Go in and decorate his office with streamers and posters, and hang a big banner that says, "My Dad is Number One!"
29. Write him a Bible verse every day, tape it to his steering wheel, and talk to him about it when he gets home.
30. Make a list of some of the major things he has done for me, and why I appreciate each one.
31. Ask him to help me make a list of the qualities I need to look for in dates and in my future husband.
32. Take him out to lunch and pick up the bill.

God and I worked through the plan, which included lots of notes, hugs, phone calls, surprises, times together, special treats, and prayers. I figured that if one note was special, fifty would be even more special. And no one can ever get (or give) enough hugs! They are some of the best ammunition we have, through Christ, in the Christian fight.

I kept updating, adding to, and changing my action plan through the next year. "I love you" was the basis for all I did...and still do.

I really think Dad was so taken off guard that he didn't even know what to do. He was so grateful for everything! He never knew that I had a special plan (as a matter of fact, he never will), but he simply recognized the love that motivated the actions. That love has been returned to me tenfold, and it just keeps bouncing back and forth between us!

The changes in our relationship were fast, fun, and permanent. I don't have to write out the action plan anymore. Now it's in my heart. Dad and I have the most incredible relationship now. Hugs, notes, "I love you's," and good times together just come naturally.

After twelve months, I received the following note from my Dad:

Brooke, today as I was traveling on the plane, I saw a little girl. She reminded me of you when you were younger. I began to think about how much I appreciated you, not so much for all the things you have done, but for the person you are. Brooke, I admire that person, and I love that person. Your love has also shown your Mom and me how to love each other better. I'm proud to be your Daddy.

It's weird that in college I usually have more fun with my parents than with my sorority sisters, friends, and fraternity brothers, but it's true. When the pressure is on, I go home and hang out with Mom and Dad. Since my college is in my hometown, I have really gotten to share some special times with both. My friends think I'm crazy because, before I go to any sorority function (formals, parties, hayrides, etc.), I always take my dates by my house to meet Mom and Dad. It's amazing how different a guy treats you after he has met your parents!

Every Monday, Dad and I eat lunch together. And every Wednesday, Mom and I eat together. No exceptions! That's our time together, and nothing is allowed to come between it. It's so much fun!

The entire heart of our family has radically changed. We've always had a close family (even in rough times), but now there is a deeper love and joy that binds us like glue. We have the best times.

So, what started out as an obligation has turned into an incredible joy. There is nothing in the world I would trade for the relationships that have developed. My parents are some of God's greatest gifts to me.

A DIFFERENCE

Last night my mom and I were shopping (with the money I made working at K-Mart). We had the worst argument the day before, and I was feeling badly. We both had said a lot of stupid things. The store had a little teddy bear that said, "Mom, You're #1." I just had to get it.

When I gave it to Mom, the glow that went across her face made my eyes fill with tears.

Just to think that one year earlier I had wanted to kill myself. I'm so glad I didn't die. I would have missed so much. God has blessed me with so many good things. Now that I'm a year older, I realize how fortunate I am.

I bought a Kenny Marks tape for my birthday. He sings, "If there's only one thing I can do, I'll make a difference to you." I know He will. And now I know that I will too.

8

OUT OF THE PIT

David was definitely the "runt of the litter." His hand-me-down clothes must have dragged the ground when he went outside to work on the farm. Although his brothers were big, handsome, and outwardly gifted, David was small, pale, and overlooked.

In one of the most historical moments in biblical history, God spoke to the prophet Samuel and instructed him to find a new king of Israel. Samuel was guided to the house of Jesse in Bethlehem. First Jesse presented to Samuel his two oldest, most handsome, most talented sons, Eliab and Abinadab. Samuel said, "No, they won't do, for man looks at the outward appearance, but God looks at the heart." All of Jesse's available sons were presented to Samuel, but all were turned down. As a last resort, they went to the pasture to find the little reject, David.

When David was finally presented to Samuel, God said, "He's the one."

The rest is history. David continued to endure hardship, and he continued to be blessed. He spoke on behalf of all young warriors of all time when he said this about God: "He brought me out of the pit of destruction, out of the miry clay, and He set my feet upon a rock, making my footsteps firm. And He put a new song in my mouth, a song of praise to our God; many will see and fear, and he will trust in the Lord" (Psalm 40:2-3).

When man lets me down, David was saying, the Lord will pick me up.

A FRIEND IN THE MIRROR

The day started out like every day had for the past eight months. The alarm went off, and I debated whether or not I should get out of bed. I had spent another night with no sleep. I could barely move because I had consumed a box of laxatives the night before. Dizzy and cramped with pain, I inched my way into the bathroom where I hung over the toilet, nauseated for thirty minutes. I fell into a corner of the shower and just let the hot water run over me. I lay there on the shower floor cursing myself. My soul ached, but I could not cry. My face ached because I wanted to cry, but no tears would come.

I continued to lie there scheming about how I would avoid eating that day so no one would learn my secret. I started to get up but I couldn't muster enough energy. I wanted to yell for help, but I didn't think I deserved any help. Finally, I pulled myself up and looked in the mirror above the sink. I saw nothing but my pale ugliness. I hated my body so much I couldn't even look at it, but even more I hated what was inside me. "Please, God, let today be the end! Do You even hear me, God? Do You care?"

That was me—one year ago. I had a combination eating disorder of bulimia and anorexia. I stopped eating, or I vomited whatever I did eat. (I felt guilty if I even ate a carrot stick, because I wanted desperately to be thinner.) I ran up to six miles a day and did aerobics whenever I could. I took laxatives, sometimes up to fifty a day. Very few people knew of my secret habit that was slowly killing me. On the outside I was a confident, happy, outgoing, sensitive, and involved student at a top university, but on the inside I felt miserable, scared, insecure, unlovable, dirty, and fake. I held leadership positions in my church, sorority, and the

Baptist Student Union. I seemed to have it all together, but I was falling apart inside. Logically I knew that what I was doing to my body was wrong, but the guilt I had just confirmed my feeling that I really was a problem-ridden, bad person. I knew lots of facts about God. I knew that He knew who I was, but I figured He probably couldn't stand me.

I went to lots of places for help. I tried to tell my parents, but they wouldn't believe me. Then I went to a medical doctor on campus who just put me on a diet so I would at least lose weight the healthy way. My dizzy spells became more frequent, and I started taking sleeping pills just to get me through the nights. My weight was diminishing.

Finally, a friend pointed me toward a counselor who saw me for six months free of charge. He taught me about unconditional love and helped me to look at my insecurities, but the cycle kept going. Any rejection or even the slightest hint of failure drove me more into my own little world. A new doctor placed me on potassium supplements because my body was seriously lacking it. I couldn't stop being obsessed with food, exercise, and weight. I desperately wanted to feel loved and worthy. People tried to communicate their love to me, but I wasn't listening. I knew I needed God, but I couldn't find Him. And I figured that if I did find Him, even He couldn't help me.

In March my counselor explained to my parents that I needed hospitalization. Against my resistance, I was taken out of school and placed in an eating disorder unit in a hospital. There I discovered that my eating disorder was more than just a desire to be thin; it was my coping mechanism in life. I had to look at the issues *behind* the food and weight. The counselors there tried to help me determine these issues, but I wasn't honest with them. I was in a lot of denial, so I just skimmed the surface of issues and concentrated my energy on protecting myself and my family.

After six weeks I left the hospital. I did great for a couple of months, but my problems kept surfacing. I went to individual therapy and back to my groups. Slowly I opened up, and began admitting the issues I needed to deal with: perfectionism, a desperate need for my parents' approval, trust, and sexual abuse which I had kept secret for fourteen years. I decided to stay out of school that fall semester so I could deal with these issues. I had a very compassionate, caring therapist who constantly reminded me that I am okay as a person no matter what I do or who I know.

But even with all the therapy and groups, I still lacked peace, and my insecurity was as real as ever. Therapy helped me to recognize and begin to work on several problems, but it wasn't the total answer. I was becoming more and more depressed. I went to church searching for God. I read His word trying to find the answers.

Finally I turned to a girl who had pursued me since I first went into the hospital. She had conquered an eating disorder herself, and offered hope to me. She was straightforward with me: She said she could tell I knew a lot about God, but she saw that I was missing God's message of *grace*. She said I had not totally given myself and my problems to Christ.

I was angry at her for telling me this. I thought she just didn't understand how hard it was. But no—*I* was the one who didn't understand. I thought God could only see my sins and failures. She taught me that God doesn't even see my failures and wrongdoings because Christ died for all of them on the cross. That's grace—I really didn't deserve life, but Christ loved me so unconditionally that He gave His life for me so I could have a personal, intimate, trusting relationship with Him. Only a realization of this grace could bring me the peace I needed. I knew about God's grace, but I didn't live in a daily understanding of it. My eating disorder and the issues behind it did not immediately vanish, but I had finally reached a turning point.

I began to meditate on the meaning of God's word. I didn't concentrate on verses that said I am to be someone or do something, but on verses that communicated who I am in Christ, such as 2 Corinthians 5:17— "Therefore if anyone is in Christ, he is a new creation; the old has gone, the new has come!" This became a verse with new meaning for me. I claimed myself as a new creation every day. I began to see how Christ's grace really is sufficient for me. I began to understand the power Christ has. I truly believed that Christ was strengthening, restoring, and establishing me, and that He is doing that even today.

I still struggle sometimes with feeling inadequate and unworthy, and there are times when I struggle with food and exercise. But I can better recognize Satan's lies about my value and worth. I'm learning to claim that I am God's treasure and that my life is worth everything to Him. That's why Christ died—that's what grace really is. Now I just have to claim my treasure.

I'm back at school now and adjusting. I still have struggles, but God's grace is sufficient. With Christ I know that total healing is possible and that He desires for me to live a peaceful, happy life, following Him and accomplishing the purposes He has just for me. No longer will I just look for resources, but I will daily look to the Source—for that is where peace and fulfillment and comfort lie!

GAY BUT NOT HAPPY

From the time when I was four or five, I remember feeling a desire or an attraction for men in my life, older men who would show me attention or give me any type of encouragement.

These feelings multiplied with age and began to become a focus of mine, a focus which continued for over twenty years and still in some fashion continues today.

The problems started when adolescence began. Those desires for a father figure, for someone to love and protect me, changed to sexual desires, desires which I in no way understood. Being a young Christian (I had accepted Christ at the age of eleven), I knew these desires were in conflict with the Bible and with what I saw around me.

There were nights, many sleepless nights, in which I would cry myself to sleep, begging God to change me and change my desires, or just take all of my desires away. I wanted anything that would bring relief from this terrible pain.

After a couple of years of asking God to take these desires away, and realizing that they were only increasing, I decided I would give in to them in a way that would harm no one—even myself, so I thought. I began getting engrossed in pornography, hoping that by viewing women in this form it would bring out the "natural" desires down inside. Instead it only culminated in a disgust for the female body. I moved from "soft" porn to more hard-core porn, which eventually brought bisexuality, homosexuality, and bestiality into the picture and presented them as viable options.

During this time, my parents' view was that my room was my territory, and they would not invade my space. By my senior year in high school I had one large trash bag full of pornography.

I really don't think anyone knew what was going on in my heart and soul at that time. My heart and soul were dying, but on the outside I was able to maintain the ideal image of a young man. I was honored as all-conference offensive and defensive tackle, captain of the football team, member of the National Honor Society, senior class vice-president, and leader in my church youth group.

During college I was active in my local church's collegiate ministry, as well as in a nationally known parachurch group, but no one knew that almost every day for over three years I had been involved in anonymous homosexual activity at a public restroom on my university campus. This pattern of activity continued off and on for three more years.

During these six years my life was probably as close as possible to hell on earth. Each time I was with someone I gave a little more of my soul away. There were long periods of time in which I was nothing more than a vacuum which drew anything or anyone nearby into it, to try to fill the incredible ache in my soul that would not disappear. Each homosexual encounter would provide momentary relief that would quickly pass, and leave an even greater pain waiting to be dealt with. It was a continual downward spiral which involved contracting a serious sexually transmitted disease over the course of over 1,000 encounters, and being robbed twice. The second time the Lord brought me to my knees.

During this period of my life I prayed to God, asking for help and deliverance. I attended seminars which promised healing from homosexuality, and I shared my struggle with close friends, hoping they might have answers for me. They offered prayer and emotional support which I feel carried me through this time.

It's now been almost a year since my last involvement in the homosexual lifestyle. I have been involved in a ministry which places worshiping Christ and loving others before self as the most important things a Christian can do.

One of the hardest lessons for me to learn was that obedience to Christ and His commands was the most important act of worship I could do! Because of my serious emotional hurt and pain, I felt that Christ could not expect obedience from me because there was no strength inside to love myself or others. Little did I know that there was no strength because I was not allowing the Holy Spirit to work because of my sin. I believe that I am alive and well today only because of the prayers of righteous friends, the mercy of Christ, and the never-ending commitment of my closest friends to see me through this valley.

I am learning that obeying Christ, placing others' needs before my own, and attempting to love others even when I don't feel they deserve it, is bringing me freedom from a lifestyle which consumed over ten years of my life. Christ has set me free from slavery in the pit of hell on earth, and allowed me to experience both the joys and pains of life— something my lifestyle had numbed me to in the last few years of my homosexual involvement. One thing Christ has shown me is that no matter how long we stray and how far we go, Christ will kneel down wherever we are and pick us up and carry us away.

There is no one who can even think about loving me the way Christ loves me. After ten years of pursuing the "love of men," I am being freed to receive the love of Christ through some very godly, caring men in my life. There is a long journey ahead which might even someday include marriage. I am convinced that no matter how long and tough the road, Christ will be there to carry me through—and that someday, all my desires will be fulfilled in heaven.

ADDICTED AT BIRTH

I was born addicted to cocaine, and until the age of seven years I was frequently raped and abused.

Before I was a year old, my natural parents were divorced. My father went away and my mother was left with me. My mother then got into cocaine addiction and was remarried.

My stepfather had a daughter who was five years older than I. My new sister wasn't very fond of me. She would hit me and bite me until I would bleed. When all of this was taking place, my parents would be wasted on drugs or asleep.

When I was four years old, a babysitter raped me and my parents didn't even care. They just said, "He wants to be your friend."

A couple of months later, my mother was pregnant. She had a baby boy. The baby had a lot of problems with his hearing due to the cocaine. He went through several operations. When my brother was let out of the hospital, my stepfather and mother started back on the drugs. My brother and I were left to fend for ourselves. I had to feed, bathe, dress, and change him. Both of us were sick half the time because of lack of food, or eating food that was spoiled.

When I was five years old I caught pneumonia and was down to forty pounds. I was hospitalized. Before my hospitalization I had consumed quite a bit of cocaine from it being left out, and at the hospital my stomach was pumped several times.

At five-and-a-half I was selling cocaine to the people who would come to buy. You would get a password from them, see the money, then take them to the back room and show them the goods. Sometimes the people who would buy from me would give me a little for myself. So I was becoming extremely addicted to the cocaine.

If I was a good little sales girl, at the end of the month there would be a little present—so I learned to keep my mouth shut.

My mother was slowly coming off her addiction. She moved away from my stepfather and took my brother and me with her. A few years later she got remarried, and her cocaine use was only every once in a while.

During this time my real dad had remarried, and he had a little baby girl. I had to start visiting them every other weekend. My stepmother didn't like me. She would lock me in a closet or ignore me. I hated her, I hated their little girl, and I hated my father. So I couldn't wait to go home to my mother.

While my mother was married to her third husband, he stole a lot of money from me and my mom. While this was going on, my second stepdad died. I think it was due to cocaine. My mom, my new stepfather, and my brother and I went to the funeral. The funeral was open-casket. He just lay there—still, lifeless, dead. I felt so helpless. I kissed his forehead. It was like cement. That was it. I totally lost it. That night I took my mother's friend's free-base kit. I lit it up and took a long drag. I sat back and waited for it to hit. I fell asleep and dreamed of heaven, then all went black and hell was all around me. I was seven years old, and I made up my mind I wasn't ever going to touch that stuff again.

I accepted God in my heart last year. I was 13. With God in my life I have no anger, no pain, and no regrets. In some ways I'm glad of my past experience. I've learned from it. Now with the help of God, I can teach people and tell them about my life! I plan to keep going forward and to make something of my life. But I can't do it without the power of Jesus Christ, our blessed Lord!

LET GO

How can you smile when the whole world is crashing in upon you? It all started September 13 when I finally accepted Jay's invitation for me to go out with him. Since April of that year he had asked me out six different times. I kinda liked the guy, and finally told him I thought there would be no problem in trying it out for a while (knowing my father would kill me if he ever found out).

Everything was delightful and going along just great. (By the way, I'm a Christian, and I thought this guy was too.) We did things together. We had sexual boundaries, but I know he loved me, and I loved him too—I honestly did. We went to a youth rally with our youth group and grew closer together, and closer to God.

It was really great until November. I felt like a real loser, I mean. Jay was right there to support me and encourage me and tell me that I wasn't a loser and that he loved me. Because I didn't hear anything like that from anyone but him, I couldn't accept it. How could I believe him when he said I was beautiful, while at the same time my family was telling me to lose weight? I'm five-feet, three inches tall, weigh 140 pounds, and I'm beautiful? Give me a break! Meanwhile he's five-feet-six and weighs 138.

I was in a very depressed state. Sharon, a dear friend of mine, told me that Jay would almost be in tears when she would talk with him because he felt he couldn't do anything for me.

My relationship with Jay was based on talking; we talked about everything, including problems between the two of us. I guess he couldn't handle all the pressure.

Pretty soon Jay wasn't showing up for youth group or church or play practice. Two days before the performance, he dropped out of the play. He said he was failing science and really couldn't continue. I blew my top. How did he have such nerve? I couldn't believe it! I was feeling betrayed and really lonesome, afraid all the things we shared would soon end.

I guess I handled the situation childishly. I ignored him the next day at school (he hadn't shown up for church all day, didn't come over, and hadn't even called).

On Sunday my friend saw him flirting with a girl at the ice rink. Yet he couldn't come to church? I was confused!

On Monday night I felt guilty for having acted so childish and ignoring him (he didn't even look at me all day). I called him from the mall to tell him I was sorry. Expecting to hear an "Apology accepted" and an "I'm sorry, too," I was struck numb by his reply. He said, "I think we should cool it; I don't feel like having people nag me, and I just don't want to go out with you anymore."

Talk about a hard blow! I mean, here I was standing in the mall, tears literally running down my face, hurt as anything, and hearing words I never dreamed would ever be said. I hung up, went looking for my folks in the mall, and after a long search found them. Mom asked if I had seen Jay, as she had just seen him and his mom. Jay lives about a mile and a half from the mall. He had been Christmas shopping for his sister.

So on with another search. I walked up and down the halls of that mall three times and saw no trace of Jay. Looking around for my folks again, I saw Jay about five feet from the exit door. I called him three times before he heard me. He turned around and said, "Hi. It's better this way for both of us. Bye!" Another shock—I was expecting, "Sorry, I'm really sorry."

A couple of days later, December 7 to be exact, I went to a Campus Life Super Club. The topic was self-esteem, exactly what I needed. After all, I was already feeling like a loser even before my boyfriend dropped me like nothing special. Now I was sure I was a big failure.

Going home, I realized I was in more of a depressed state than when I arrived at the club. I also saw that I was a perfect example of what the club speaker was talking about. He said there are people who think they are failures, people who think that if they left the face of the earth, no one would care... Hey, that was me!

I went home. I felt nothing; I felt like nothing mattered anymore. I really was empty inside. It's hard to explain. I started taking pills, not realizing what I was doing (I was trying to overdose). I didn't know how many pills to take.

I'm still alive today because Jesus cares. He woke me up and made me realize that all this time I had not put the situation in His hands. I had said, "Lord, all this bad stuff is going wrong in my life, and You tell me to just let go? You tell me that if I leave it all in Your hands, Someone who I can't even see, that You'll take care of it? You must be crazy!"

But anything is better than going through what I was going through. So I finally let go. I finally said, "Lord, it's all yours. I'm trusting You to do something."

I'm alive today, and I praise and thank God for my life. If it were not for Him, I would be lying six feet under the ground.

I also thank God that today Jay and I are friends—not like we were before, but we are good friends. It'll probably remain that way. But God works everything out for the best if you lay it all in His hands. Lay your burdens down at the cross, and He will take you the rest of the way.

Of course we all have trials. But don't give up. That's when you have to try. Don't be like Jay, who said, "I'm almost done trying!" That won't get you anywhere.

If you are questioning God, give Him a try. I promise that God won't fail you!

9

WHEN GOD
IS AT HIS BEST

Job probably suffered more than any other man in history. It went on for years. His friends told him, "Bad things happen to bad people, so you must be bad." Job listened and began to agree that bad things just can't happen to good people.

But Job had one good friend named Elihu who spoke for God. Elihu said, "You're both wrong. Bad things happen to everyone. They're not pointless, but they purify us."

In the end, Job was twice as good and twice as humble as he was before he suffered, and God was honored.

Perhaps Paul the apostle, who carried the gospel to the world in the earliest days of Christianity, showed it best. What a man Paul was! As he traveled from town to town, his Holiday Inn was usually the city jail. Instead of getting a massage before bed, his back was often laid open with a whip. He received swimming lessons in the open ocean, adrift at sea. His favorite recreation was hundred-mile hikes in his sandals down dusty roads.

Paul was tough as nails. He also had a physical handicap that he called a thorn in his flesh. Three times Paul asked God to take it from him. Three times God said, "No, Paul. I'm more powerful if you're more weak. I'm at my best when you're humble. My grace is all you need." Paul humbly replied, "I glory in my sufferings. I boast in my afflictions. I know that God will cause all things to work together for my good if I love Him, for I am called according to His purpose."

LAUGHING ON THE OUTSIDE

Growing up I was full of deep-seated bitterness and anger toward my mom and dad. I felt that I could never measure up to what they wanted me to be. I felt distant from my family, like I just didn't belong.

I realize I didn't come into this world under the best of circumstances; my mom got pregnant when she was a twenty-year-old college student. The guy she was dating at the time—my natural father—wasn't the man she desired to marry because they simply didn't love each other; they barely even knew each other. While my mom was carrying me she met another guy, and after I was born, they got married. He had been recently divorced and had a two-year-old girl.

I knew growing up that my older sister had a different mom, but I just assumed that my dad was my natural father; no one had told me otherwise. But you know, it's amazing what a little kid can sense. I knew that something was different between my dad and me. There was a special bond my dad had with his daughter that wasn't there between him and me. I didn't understand it, so as I grew older I thought it must be something I was doing wrong. I desired so much to be Daddy's Little Girl, but it just never happened. Eventually I gave up trying.

My mom and I didn't seem to communicate well either. I couldn't figure out why Mom and I didn't connect. I thought maybe it was because I was such a tomboy. Nothing gave me as much joy as being outside bike-riding, climbing trees, getting covered in mud, and building a good fort with my buddies. Playing dress-up or house or even wearing dresses just didn't do anything for me. I knew this frustrated my mom and that it seemed to put more distance between us. The distance made me withdraw deeper within myself, and I learned to deal with things by burying my feelings behind walls that I built brick by brick.

The ability to hide my true feelings, to hold back tears, and to fake being happy started a very, very unhealthy trend in my life (a trend that became the hardest area for me to change later on). I began to see myself as someone who wasn't worth much to anyone unless I could prove myself. I became a performance-oriented person outside my home, which was interesting. I guess that was because in my eyes I would never be what my folks wanted, so why try? At school, however, I could make people laugh, and I seemed to have the ability to make my teachers smile and respond to me in a positive way. I was well liked, and on the outside I seemed like a happy kid, full of life and spunk. However, inside I was hurting like a wounded puppy longing to be held.

At the age of fourteen I found out, through an argument with my older sister, that I had another father. Finding out that the man I had called Dad for fourteen years wasn't my natural father threw me for a loop. But realizing that this information had been kept from me for so long, and that I had found out by accident, and especially that no one seemed to *care* how I would feel about it—all this made me really angry. My natural father knew I had been born, and knew I was his only child on this earth, yet he made no attempt whatsoever to get to know me until after I found out about him. More than ever I just felt like a misfit and a huge mistake.

Soon afterward I got the chance to meet this new man in my life. I met him beside a pay phone at a shopping mall. I had no idea what to expect. The only thing I knew was that we looked alike, and I knew his name. As I stood in the mall waiting for him, I wondered if he would be disappointed because I wasn't the daughter he wanted me to be. Not only had I set myself up to fail, but I went into that relationship with my walls built and my heart hardened. My natural father and I tried to build some kind of a father-daughter relationship, but I was too closed, and he was too determined to change me to fit his image of what I should be, which pushed me further away from him. *Why does my family always want to change me? What's wrong with me? Why can't they just accept me for who I am?* These were some of the questions that haunted me as I lay in bed at night fighting back tears.

The years to come would be the hardest so far in my life. I went through a period of depression that no one knew about. I became a pro at hiding my emotions. Not a day went by that I didn't entertain thoughts of suicide, from as early as eighth grade until I was a junior in high school.

I got involved with Young Life in high school as a social activity. Even though I met some neat people, this Man they called Jesus just seemed like some fairy tale. I couldn't understand how the love He had to offer could fill the hole inside me. I couldn't see Him or touch Him, so how could they expect me to believe He really existed? I kept going to their meetings because we played fun games and got to go on trips. One of those trips would later change my life.

When I was a junior, things in my life came to a breaking point. I was tired of feeling I'd never amount to anything. I seemed to be more distant from my family than ever, and my natural father and I were beginning to clash with each other all the time. I wanted to give up on life. There just wasn't anything worth staying around for. It was then that I tried to take my life by overdosing on assorted pills.

It was a Friday, and I had just gone through a week of let-downs. I had hurt someone I loved dearly by some lies I told, a person who had poured so much love into me. She was my P.E. teacher, and I was afraid her love for me wouldn't last, now that I had tested her love and it had backfired. My goal in life at that time was to be accepted by this lady, and for her to love me for who I was. I tested her that week by telling her a dangerous lie about my mother, and because she cared for me so much she believed me.

The lie I created became a monster. When my teacher found out the truth, it crushed her, and she cried. That broke my heart. I remember being so mad at myself for not being able to trust the love she had for me, and for not realizing that her love was for real. I had proved to myself that I was a jerk, that I was no good to anyone. I always seemed to hurt people, and I convinced myself I would be better off dead and out of the way.

I went home early that day and attempted to O.D. But an amazing thing happened after I had taken all those pills. I was standing in the kitchen, feeling like my stomach was being stomped on, when I became tingly all over and my vision blurred. I was really frightened. For the first time I was afraid to die, and I decided to do anything I could to stay alive. I went back to school (guided by angels, I know), and some friends of mine rushed me to the hospital, where I passed out. When I woke up, my P.E. teacher was holding my hand with tears running down her face. My mom, on the other hand, kept her distance and let me know how disappointed she was in me. The one time I needed my mom to hold me, and even would have allowed her to do so, she kept her distance—and so did I.

My natural father tried to use my suicide attempt as a way of feeding his theory that he should be raising me, and that he could make me into what I should be. The man I considered my dad thought the suicide attempt was my way of embarrassing the family. My aunt simply said, "We won't tell your grandmother what you did...it would break her heart." To this day she doesn't know.

So I went on with my life in a deeper hole than I was in before I attempted suicide. A turning point came during spring break that year down at Padre Island when I met an incredible 87-year-old lady called Pardner. She simply loved me, and was willing to listen to my heart. We would get up early and go on the beach together to collect sea shells and sand dollars. She would just smile at me for no reason, as she held on to my arm. I couldn't figure out why this lady who didn't know anything about me was so willing just to love me for who I was. She could see I was hurting, but didn't force me to open up. I kept on waiting for her to try some tactic to get me to spill my guts and break down my walls. But all she did was spend time with me and spend love on me. I was floored! I was also curious to know what she was all about.

Pardner told me about this man named Jesus, who I had heard so much about in Young Life. But most of all she showed me what love was by her actions. For the first time I was beginning to understand this love that Jesus had to give me. Pardner was a walking, talking Jesus, and she showed me how special I was simply because God created me. There on Padre Island I invited Jesus Christ into my life, and there my inward hole began to fill, and the walls began to crack. I had finally found Someone who would love me unconditionally.

The years that followed have been filled with ups and downs, but the course of my life changed that day. No longer was I in control. It became a gradual process of getting to know Jesus as my Savior and as the Lord of my life, an everyday process of learning how to trust Him, to surrender everything to Him. It was a process of allowing Him to love me and allowing myself to love Him. It hasn't always been easy, but God is faithful and He is sovereign.

Today I can say with confidence that Jesus Christ is my best friend. He is my heavenly Daddy whom I love with all my heart. He knows my deepest thoughts and fears. He knows my shortcomings and loves me just the same. Things with my family are getting better, and I'm learning to build a bridge to shorten the distance. I'm doing that by learning how to honor and value my family, and to love them unconditionally simply because God created them and chose me to be born into this family.

I've learned over the years that I can choose to go through life full of bitterness and anger, but the bottom line is that as a Christian, regardless of my circumstances, I am responsible for how I respond to them, how I act, and how I live. I can now say with sincerity that I truly love my family. I may not agree with how they choose to live their lives or how they see me; I simply love them for who they are.

I've come a long way and I've got a long way to go, but God is so faithful. I look ahead with a smile, knowing that God is molding me and changing me and loving me so very much. That makes me smile. I look forward to getting to know my God more in the years to come, and getting to glorify Him with my life!

A SOUND MIND

I suppose in every person's life there are certain experiences from the past that come to mind every so often—things like a teenage friend's funeral, winning a state championship, your sixteenth birthday party, your grandmother's death. I, too, have had some similar experiences, but there is one experience from my past that I have literally thought of every day since it happened. Mine is somewhat unusual because it deals with mental illness.

Most people can relate to this topic, at least to some extent, because they have had relatives or friends who were mentally ill, or at least have had friends who had relatives who were mentally ill. Most Americans in their lifetime will come into contact with someone who has undergone some type of psychiatric care. However, in my case it was not a relative or close friend; it was me!

I was a student living at home with my parents. I had run away months earlier in the middle of the night, leaving behind clothes and a note that was confusing, and which exemplified the state of anxiety I had been in for weeks. What had led to the breakdown is too complicated to pen, but it should be mentioned here that by this point I had talked to everyone I thought could help me. Even the $10,000 allowed by my father's insurance policy, which I had spent at a private psychiatric clinic, had not purchased the answer to my depression and pain.

On the morning of November 4, I went to work at McDonald's at around 5:30; it was a part-time job I had taken in an attempt to get back into the flow. By 8:30 A.M. the little restaurant beside the freeway was bustling. I was working at the grill, taking heat from both the manager and the grill. This was a lot of pressure for a young guy who was still taking Tofranil, an anti-depressant drug intended to help my depressed state. By 8:45 the pressure had fully mounted, and what happened next I still do not understand. Apparently my behavior was abnormal, and when I got into an argument with another employee, I was sent home.

I arrived home some time before 10 A.M. with a young man who had been hitchhiking his way from Dallas to Florida. By this time I was overly talkative, irrational, and even violent. Unknown to me, my mother had seen this manic state coming on for days. My brother, Jason, got me in the back bedroom and made impossible attempts to calm me down as I accelerated into a full-blown manic episode. I hit my brother in the face with my fist. And though I don't remember it, my mother told me I drew back to hit her also, but for some reason didn't strike her. She then called the county judge and the East Texas Regional Mental Health Office for help.

She packed me into her car, and she and my brother-in-law drove me straight to the county seat. During the trip I talked incessantly about religious topics (this is common among manics during an episode). We drove directly to the mental health center. All three of us went into a large office to see a psychologist. This man asked me a couple of questions. He then asked my brother-in-law and me to leave the office, and we went out into the lobby to wait. Mom came out several minutes later with some papers in her hand.

We drove to the county courthouse, where we were introduced to a deputy sheriff. He immediately took us in a sheriff's car to see two different doctors who, unknown to me at the time because of my manic state, interviewed me and evaluated my mental condition. After talking to the second doctor, I was informed that I was being committed to the state mental hospital. I broke down and cried for ten minutes in the office. After the tears had been wiped away, the deputy sheriff took us back to the courthouse, where I was introduced to my court-appointed attorney. She explained to me that my mother had committed me for ninety days, an act of love that I now respect. The lawyer then explained my rights, handed me her business card, and asked me to sign a paper agreeing to the treatment. In just a few minutes a highway patrol officer took me to his car and drove me to the hospital where I was admitted to the G-ward of the acute unit.

For the next week and a half I remained at Level 4-D, which basically meant I was not allowed to leave the ward, even for meals, and my visitors were limited. During the first ten days or so I slept only four to five hours a night, and in the daytime was often unable to even sit down. Twice I was attacked by other patients; once I was hit in the face and the second time tackled to the ground. These two experiences were frightening, but in a worse experience I got violent again myself and struck one of the mental health workers. The next thing I knew, three of the workers had my hands bound and were dragging me into the seclusion room as I kicked, cursed, and screamed. While I kept fighting, they took off my boots, then left, locking the door behind them.

The room had a small window in the door. In a manic state of indescribable hyperactivity, I stared through the plexiglass window as other patients walked by, and I began screaming, "Let me out! Somebody, please let me out!" After giving up the screaming, I looked around the room: Five feet by ten feet, a window in the door, a mattress and blanket. I felt more alone at that moment than I will ever be be able to explain. I was totally alone in a hospital just sixteen miles from my hometown—the same hospital I had driven past literally hundreds of times, casually cracking jokes about its patients.

After the seclusion room experience I went through many strange side effects from a drug called Loxitane, an anti-psychotic. However, by Thanksgiving I had progressed enough to be able to go home on a five-day furlough. After the furlough, I returned to the hospital until the first week of December, when I was released.

Truly I have thought of this experience every day since I was released just nine months ago. At times I fear it might happen again, when I occasionally struggle through anxiety attacks and mood swings. And even though my pride was totally stripped away when I was forced by court order to go to a mental hospital, I can say that my personal bout with manic-depression has been the most valuable experience in my twenty-two years of life. I believe the only way I can say this with total confidence is because Jesus is my Lord.

Like anyone else who believes in God and has endured hardship, I questioned why He would let me have this condition. I was angry at God during my depressed times, and verbally abusive of my dad also. But when I began to get well, and as I slowly accepted this hereditary illness I now share with my brother, who is 26, God brought a gentle restoration of my relationship with Him as well as with my dad. I strongly believe that the prayers of my pastor, parents, college professors, and many friends sped up the healing process. I am so thankful that God in His wisdom allowed me to endure such a trial, that I might feel firsthand the healing power of His love. I am especially thankful to God for teaching me the importance of letting others help me when I am in need, instead of being too proud to receive the love of concerned friends and family. And now the peace of God, times of testing, and brotherly love are more than interesting topics discussed at a Bible study. For I have personally experienced them all.

KARA'S STORY

THE LUMP THAT BECAME A MOUNTAIN TO CLIMB

When I was a little girl sitting around a warm, peaceful campfire at summer camp one night and asked Jesus into my heart, little did I know how important and necessary that decision would be during my teenage years.

When I first noticed the small lump in my throat just above my collarbone, I really didn't think much about it. I thought it was an insect bite of some kind. Soon there were other lumps…about one new one each week. The diagnosis went from insect bite to inflamed node to mono, to cat-scratch fever, to biopsy time. I thought to myself, *No way could I have cancer!* I felt invincible.

As I came out of the anesthesia, the doctors told me the lumps looked cancerous. I was still kind of out of it, and I thought, *Whatever…*

That night I needed to study for a test, and I did. I didn't burst out crying; I said to myself, *I'm going to be rational and just deal with this.*

The next day, the cancer diagnosis was confirmed.

My friends were wonderful. They were all shocked, but totally supportive. I didn't want pity. I just wanted to be treated normally. But now my world was so different. No one would treat me the same. Then overnight the truth hit me, and I got really scared.

I went to the M. D. Anderson Clinic in Houston, where I was put through a battery of tests. They poked and prodded every inch of my body. I just put on my Walkman and listened to good music. I kept a positive attitude even though I was totally drained. The tests were fascinating. The doctors were brilliant. I was impressed. They were wonderful people and explained everything to me. The mutant cells responsible for my condition were just complicated cells that were missing one minor part.

When they decided to remove my spleen, I kept telling myself, *So many people have been through much worse. You can do it.* The worst part of the surgery was the morphine. It was like being on drugs. I've always hated drugs. I felt so out of it. They gave me a pack to take home, but I didn't use any.

Since that surgery I've had twenty-five treatments of radiation. They fried my neck and armpits. I lost some hair on the top of my neck, but that was it. The radiation makes you so tired. When I got my energy back, I couldn't believe it. A huge weight was taken off my shoulders.

I prayed a lot and thanked God that I was alive and getting well. I'm upbeat because sickness has a lot to do with attitude. I'm not afraid to die. My faith makes me a strong person. God is my best friend. I can't imagine life without Christ in the center of my heart.

ANGIE'S STORY

L.D.—"LIFE DEVELOPER"

My story starts back in second grade. I wasn't doing really well in school, and the teachers said it was because I was lazy. They told my mother they were going to hold me back a year. She told them she wanted me tested for a learning disability. Then the school tested me and said I had no problems. Well, my mother wasn't satisfied and took me to a special doctor. He tested me and told my mother I *did* have a learning disability, and it would be best to hold me back a year so I could catch up.

My parents decided that since I would be held back, we should move so it would be easier on me. We moved to a smaller town where I still live. Over the years I have struggled with my problem, and barely slid by to the next grade. This past year, my junior year, I had a D average until the last quarter. I got my grade card in the mail and was so happy: I finally got a C average.

I'm telling all of this because it was during that last quarter of school that I really began trusting in the Lord with everything. The Lord was there for me when I needed Him.

I used to wonder why the Lord would allow me to have this problem, but now I know. He allowed it for this reason: so I could tell my story and maybe help others through their problems too. I know now that if you put your faith in the Lord, He will come through for you in your time of need. That's why during my senior year I am going to make the best grades ever, because I have my Lord Jesus Christ there with me. He's with me everywhere I go. Even in a little town of 5,000 people.

He's also there for *you,* wherever you are.

I pray for you and wish you the best of luck with your life and L.D. problems, however bad they may be.

> *"For the mountains may be removed and the hills may shake, but My lovingkindness will not be removed from you, and My covenant of peace will not be shaken," says the Lord who has compassion on you. (Isaiah 54:10)*

10

AT THE END
OF THE END

From the lips of the great Teacher Himself, Jesus Christ, came these words: "God causes the sun to shine on the evil and on the good, and sends rain on the righteous and the unrighteous." God is not out of control. He hasn't lost His grip on the world's events. Although He is not the creator of evil, God does give us freedom to choose evil over good. He allows our evil choices to take their toll, but He always has the last say. He speaks for eternity—with eternal rewards for the godly and eternal punishment for the ungodly.

An accident caused by a drunk driver took the life of my very good friend Dennis Carruth, as well as the life of his baby. It still hurts all of us who loved Dennis. God didn't make that other driver drunk. But He allowed that man the freedom to sin. Now Dennis and his baby are in Paradise preparing to assist in the celebration as each of his friends arrives safely home. No evil is too horrible for God to set straight.

It is always humbling and embarrassing to tell about it, but my biggest downfall happened in my marriage. At Southern Methodist University, I married a brown-eyed doll named Cindy Lynch. Yes, I loved her and planned to spend the rest of my life with her. I was also a little too concerned with my personal glory in a game called football, and spent too much time looking for myself in the *Dallas Morning News* on Sunday mornings. (Usually I was at the bottom of the pile... What was I looking for anyway?) The day I graduated, our troubles began. I went to our sports camp to work with kids and coach football at

Texas A&M, and she left—with my best friend—permanently. Wow! Was I devastated! Divorce doesn't just hurt; it destroys.

Man, I was at the end of the end. I cried out to God. And He answered. His answer wasn't what I asked for; it was infinitely *better*. My tears turned into splendor. After I cried for a few dark months, He introduced me to a girl-wonder named Debbie-Jo. Eighteen months later, a box of Cracker Jacks she was eating had a diamond ring in the surprise package. (Amazing, huh?) Six months after that, I caught her in a wedding gown walking down the aisle of a church into my arms. I still can't get over it. Eighteen years have gone by, and I'm helplessly in love. I have butterflies when we kiss. We hold hands and my pulse does a rap beat. Four incredible kids call me Dad (and other stuff, sometimes). My favorite vacation spot is my home. My best playmates are my wife and kids. It's crazy, but it's good.

God hates divorce! But God takes even a miserable sinner like me and turns my sadness into dancing. He's an amazing God. I'm always in awe of how He keeps up with all of the broken pieces; he somehow finds a puzzle with just one missing piece to fit us perfectly into.

Dark nights end with an incredible sunrise.

Mine did—and so will yours!

THROUGH ALL THE MUD

For many years before I accepted Christ, Satan brought me through all the mud he could find. From age 8 to 13, I was mentally and sexually abused by my cousin, who was in his early twenties. What made it worse was that my aunt and uncle knew about it and allowed it right in front of them, while they got high and drank themselves crazy. In the fourth grade I was diagnosed as being manic-depressive. (It's a kind of chemical imbalance; at times I would be higher than the birds, happy and content with life, but the next minute I might be lower than low).

My mom and dad and I always fought. My mom is a perfectionist, and even at six years of age I was required to have nothing wrong with my appearance or surroundings. She constantly yelled at me, like you yell at a dog.

I grew up with terribly low self-esteem. By the sixth grade I was already smoking and trying alcohol. Then I went through a period of thinking I was fat because my mother was always very weight-conscious. I became anemic and was like a toothpick in the eighth grade. I tried to commit suicide by taking a bottle of pills in the bathroom at school. The teachers made me throw up, and they sent me to the emergency room. I was dismissed from school for a week and a half for counseling. I became furious and rebellious, even more than before.

I began smoking again and drinking every once in a while. In my ninth-grade year my great aunt and my great grandpa died, two of the closest people to me. I became angry at God. Oh yes, I was very aware of God; my parents were sorta Christians, but my grandparents, who practically raised me, were sold out for Jesus Christ. (There were many times I wanted to call Grandma "Mom.")

My life went downhill that fall. I was hooked on cigarettes and more angry at God, blaming Him for everything. I fell in love with a boy my sophomore year. He was a senior, and we were head over heels for each other. He was a Christian, but I wasn't, and Satan used me to pull him down. He began to drink a lot. After five months, when it was close to Christmas and he was going to get me a promise ring, I found out he had slept with one of my drunk friends who I had thought was so terrific.

My boyfriend and I broke up; two days after Christmas I tried to commit suicide again. It was 1:30 A.M. and my mother was awake and feeling disturbed. She walked in and found the suicide note as I started to slit my wrists. She grabbed me and we fought. Finally she screamed and my father ran in and held me down. They stayed in my room for the next week or so while I slept.

I started drinking at school and after work, during the week and on weekends. I was always very conscious of my figure and looks, and had no problem getting dates. But little did I realize I was using guys to try to fill a void in my life, and to try to change my perspective of myself. Since I had been abused, I grew up thinking that the only way I could be accepted and loved was to offer my body.

By the end of that year I was so miserable. I would get drunk and not remember what happened. I would wake up with a hangover from coming in at 5 A.M. and passing out on my aunt's couch (I stayed at her house when I was working a late shift; I was supposed to be home from work by one). She prayed for me all the time, but I seemed to be in my own world, and no one could reach me.

My parents took me to a Christian counselor. He worked with me for three years and never gave up on me, showing me, by the way he lived, an example of how Christ won't give up on you or me. I became like an addition to his family—the daughter he never had—to add to his two sons and beautiful wife. Together, we were like a complete family of God. My life began turning around.

Near the end of my junior year I began giving up again. My mom kicked me out of the house. My life seemed a big zero. I cried so much. Life seemed hopeless and useless. My dad came to me a week and a half later, crying and asking me to come home. He told me he loved me. Daddy was bigger than life to me, and I loved him so much. I truly loved my mother too, but she was always jealous of me. She had me when she was very young, and never knew how to be my mom.

Then one Sunday I stumbled into church with a hang-over. The people began giving testimonies of how Christ changed their lives. Then it happened: My heart was just completely broken down, and conviction came in. I walked up to the front, crying the whole way, and got in front of my pastor and said, "I need to make a commitment to Christ, and I need to say something to the church."

I stood there and humbled myself before the church and Christ. When I got through, there wasn't a dry eye in the whole auditorium. Every one of those people had been praying for me (I do believe in prayer!). That day I became like a quiet, peaceful child with the beauty of Christ inside.

This is my senior year, and sober life has been wonderful. (My relationship with my mother has been healed too.) In May it will be one year that I've gone without alcohol. You know, this year has been great, but it's also been the normal struggle. In fact, it's been unbearable at times, but Christ's strength has come shining through stronger than anything. Alcohol, drugs, and sex can give you a feeling of highness and pleasure, but heaven will give you pleasure and a high that will last not just overnight, but eternally. Life is worth living!

Though I've been through a lot of pain in my life, I don't want pity or a feeling of, "Oh, I'm so sorry you went through that." I praise God that I did go through it, and that I came out with some knowledge so I can hopefully help others. I want my life to be an example of Christ.

Remember, people will always hurt you and let you down, but God will never give up on you or fail you. I am just so thankful for being restored again; things are so much better. If you have problems, turn them over to God. It's senseless to fight a battle that God has already won.

PRACTICAL PRIORITIES

Last August I lost the most important person in my life—my Aunt Ruth. It's hard to explain what she meant to me. I have grown up in a tight, close-knit family that is full of love. This aunt was 72. When I was born, she was our only relative who had the time to keep children during the day and on weekends. She lived only four or five miles from us, so it was easy for my parents to take me to her house. When I was younger I spent two or three afternoons a week at her house, as well as about five weekends each year.

Last June her health declined greatly. She could no longer get out of bed without help, or walk more than eight to twelve feet without resting. When I left for summer camp in July, I was praying several times a day for her, hoping she would be better when I returned. I came home and found her bedridden in a hospital bed and needing full-time help. I was with her for at least an hour almost every day in August, whether she was in the hospital or at home.

Five days after school started late that month, I was in the middle of my first test when I was called into the office. My dad told me of her death. For twenty-four hours I was in a state of emotional shock, crying for an hour, in a daze for an hour, back and forth like that, not eating, drinking, or talking—it was horrible!

For the next three or four months I lost faith in every-thing: God, the power of prayer, friends, and family. I didn't care anymore. In November I went with a church group to Washington D.C. and New York City. The group leaders showed me it was not my fault. (I blamed myself for not being with her the morning she died, thinking I could have done something). These leaders showed me that God still cared; He did not desert me. It was time for my aunt to go to be with God, and for me to entrust myself and my future to Him. He would pull me through and take care of me.

If I have one thing to tell people, it's this: Don't ever give up faith, whatever happens. He will pull you through if you trust Him completely. I am just now starting to pray regularly and trust God in everything. Please listen: The power of prayer will never be surpassed and will always amaze you. Don't waste the time I did. Keep your priorities in line: God first, and then the other important things in your life. I had mine like this: Aunt Ruth, God, family, and so forth. It took her death to allow me to see this, and to correct it.

CINDY'S STORY

APPETITE FOR SELF-DESTRUCTION

When I was as young as eight years old, I can remember feeling fat. In baby pictures I had a round belly, and then as a little girl I still had baby fat. By the time I was in third grade I had lost my stomach and was thin—not because I had dieted but because I had simply outgrown the fat. Yet I still couldn't let go of the feelings that I was fat. I never tried to lose weight in elementary school, but when I was 13 and in the eighth grade, I saw a movie about a closet bulimic. I decided that looked like a good way to get thin, so I tried it. It was so disgusting to make myself throw up that I decided I would diet instead.

I began skipping desserts and not eating between meals. Throughout the first year my dieting gradually progressed without me fully realizing what was happening. Since my parents weren't at school to see me eat lunch, I began skipping it. Gradually I began eating breakfast before my dad woke up; I would put some bread crumbs on my plate and lie about my having already eaten. I would feed my dinner to my dog under the table, or not be home for dinner and say I had eaten when I hadn't.

I had been taking ballet, and now began dancing three hours every day and jogging two miles a day. I felt so guilty about eating that I had cast aside all repulsiveness at purging. I started purging once or twice a week, and before long I was throwing up four times a day. It was such a gradual but snowballing thing that I felt I had no control over it.

For as long as I can remember, people have told me I have a perfect life. I have never been in need of anything: My parents are still married; we live in a nice home; my family goes to church; and I'm a good student who's well-liked at school. I have always tried to maintain this ideal image, even while my life was falling apart on the inside.

I had been trying so hard to maintain an image of perfection that I didn't care if it cost me my life. I knew that what I was doing was unhealthy, but I couldn't seem to stop. I told myself that it wouldn't get bad, but it did. My goals had always been idealistic, but I had always been able to achieve them. I was a straight-A honor student, a good dancer, a model, and an officer in almost every club I was in. I was active in my church (though I didn't know God), and was respected by my peers and by adults. It seemed natural that this perfect girl could achieve a perfect body as well. Unfortunately, I went past the perfect body stage (though I had been relatively thin to begin with), and I soon hit the skinny, scrawny stage. Always an overachiever, I also overdid my dieting, and soon I was blacking out, having dizzy spells—and I almost died.

For four years I was anorexic and bulimic. That period of time was hell for me. Everything I did revolved around my weight. I could only go out to eat with my friends if I hadn't eaten yet and if the restaurant had a salad bar. It took me an hour every morning just to decide what to wear! I had to try on everything in the closet and pick the one thing that made me look the thinnest. I exercised constantly and purged almost everything I ate. Eventually, I reduced my food intake to 40 calories per day, and my weight dropped to 90 pounds (I'm five-foot-six).

During this time I was also depressed and wanted to kill myself. I would experiment by taking ten Tylenol or Advil tablets, or any other medication, to see how much I could take without hurting myself. Also, when I was angry at someone else, I vented my frustration on myself in this way. Cutting my wrists was another form of venting my anger. I was under the impression that good girls never got angry, and I desperately wanted to be good.

Then my whole world turned upside down. One of my best friends tried to kill herself by overdosing on Tylenol and cutting her wrists. She was in intensive care for several days and almost didn't make it. I was so angry with her and felt so guilty and upset that I vowed I would never do anything like that again myself.

In three weeks I was doing it again, and two months later I accidentally overdid it. I had taken twelve Midol tablets the night before to punish myself for having eaten too much (I had eaten one bite of chicken), and the next morning in school the medication really started affecting me. I broke out in hives, was shaking, had a very rapid pulse, and could not breathe very well. The school nurse and a guidance counselor came to my class and removed me. My parents were called and took me to a doctor who recommended I be taken to the hospital for my eating disorder.

I stayed in the hospital for three months. The doctors found I had seriously damaged my body with the anorexia and bulimia. My esophagus had been torn, my blood pressure was extremely low, I was dehydrated, and I was so malnourished that my body had begun to eat the muscle. In addition to regular meals I had to drink liquid dietary supplements every day. I underwent a lot of counseling there and continued my therapy after getting back home, but I had only improved slightly.

Seven months after leaving the hospital, I tried to kill myself. I had been taking antidepressants and overdosed on them. My doctor was furious and told me I was lucky to be alive. That's when I realized death was permanent. At that point I had been doing better with eating but was still struggling. Before this event, death and my illness hadn't scared me, but after such a close call, I was frightened.

I had been brought up in a Christian home and I knew about God, but I didn't know Him personally. If I died, I wasn't sure I would go to heaven.

During my four years of struggling, my thoughts were rarely on God. When I did think about Him, I was angry at Him for letting these things happen to me. I had several Christian friends and found myself gravitating toward them. We went to church and Young Life together, and slowly I realized that God had been there all the time, with His hand extended toward me. I had simply refused to take it.

After my suicide attempt I found I needed God to make it through even one day of eating normally. An adult friend helped me reconfirm my faith by asking Jesus into my heart. That was one and a half years ago. Since then I have been active in my Christian walk and have learned what it means to trust Christ, and how important faith is. It hasn't been easy; I have struggled a lot and have had to overcome setbacks. But with God's help I've made it further than I ever thought I would, and I've finally started to enjoy life.

11

KNOWING THE LOVE

Only a few short years ago, something happened to my youngest girl that has shaken my total being so thoroughly that I know I'll never be the same. Little Courtney (I call her Corky—it fits her bouncy little personality better) was eight (going on 17) years old. She's always a bundle of emotional energy. A new set of clothes or perfecting a new trick in gymnastics makes her squeal with excitement. If her new dress doesn't fit, she may just cry for a while.

As Courtney hit third grade math that year, she really found it tough. Her red-apple teacher, Mrs. Brown (who calls her class "big folks" when they're good), passed out a test of thirty problems (like 7 minus 4, and 6 plus 8) that had to be done in three minutes. Each student had to make 100 before they could go on.

On Monday, Courtney failed the test.

On Tuesday, Courtney failed the test again.

On Wednesday it happened a third time, and she came home crying, the pains of failure evident on her face.

That night we practiced math for an hour together. For me it was great; any excuse to spend extra time with one of my four best little buddies is like a day at Disney World for me. But for Corky it was hard. She didn't have time to count with her cute little fingers any longer. It didn't come easy for her.

The next morning we got up at 6:30 to practice some more. At four that afternoon, a sad little princess came dragging home from school. When I walked into her room, with its green carpet and flowery wallpaper, the look in her swollen red eyes told me all I needed to know about her fourth straight failure.

The stopwatch was on her desk, and four wadded-up tests were scattered across the floor. She was still trying to do it. By now her thoughts were prisoners to sadness and frustration.

"Princess," I said, to soothe her sorrow.

"Leave me alone," she snapped in haste.

"Hey, Corky, it's okay, baby. I just want to help you."

"Go away!" she persisted.

"Courtney, I don't care what your grades are on the dumb math test. I just want to be your friend."

"I don't want to talk." She made her point clear, and it hurt.

"Okay, little buddy," I spoke tenderly. "I'll leave, but I want you to know it hurts my feelings when you talk to me that way."

I didn't see Corky again until bedtime. As I walked by my bed at about 9 P.M. a small orange envelope caught my eye. My full name was written on the outside. It was a note from Courtney. I tore it open quickly and a purple sucker fell into my hand. I got the message immediately. A sucker was all she could find in her room to say, "Hey, Dad, you're special. Here's an eight-year-old's way of saying I love you."

The words didn't need to be spelled right to give me the message. I walked straight to her room, still half-amazed at her heart of gold that is always ready to say, "I'm sorry." I wanted to hold her, to tell her it's okay, to tell her how I loved her, too. Dear God, how I love my little girl!

I wasn't mad at her previous insult. I could hardly even remember the put-down. I didn't care if she wasn't perfect. She's my little girl!

In her room she was curled up asleep against her teddy bear like a warm puppy. The peace of God's blessing had wiped the tears from her eyes. As I leaned over to hold her, something happened inside my heart that will encourage me forever.

A still, small voice whispered in my inner ear: "Joe, I'm your Daddy, too." I knew God was talking to me. His voice was quiet, but I knew it was Him. He had set me up for a loving word that I needed to hear: "The love you have for Courtney is the love I have for you. When My word says, 'Your sins are forgiven,' I mean they're *forgotten.* Just let Me love you. You mean so much to Me."

I've failed in my life many, many times. I've let God down, and haven't been the man He wants me to be. But on the day I opened my heart to Him and let Him come in, He forgave me. Now I know the feeling inside that a daddy has when his child says, "I'm sorry."

Want to know that love? (I never met a kid or adult who didn't, deep inside.)

Give Him a lollipop... Tell Him you're sorry... Ask Him into your heart (*now,* if you want to), and gently close your eyes and experience a loving Father's arms around you as He says, "To as many as received Him, to them He gave the right to be a child of God" (John 1:12).

A STRONGER FAMILY

It all started on June 29 when I accepted Christ into my life at a summer camp called Kanakuk. My life up until then was as normal as that of any other 15-year-old. It was not until I asked Jesus into my life that things started to change. After being reborn and returning home, my interest in the Lord began to grow by leaps and bounds. I stopped hanging around a lot of people who brought me down. I stopped drinking, stopped messing around with girls, and even stopped cursing. I also became involved in a church youth group and a Bible study group.

Like plenty of other teenagers, I lived at home with both my parents, and I thought they were Christians because they went to church and encouraged me to do the same. But I began to realize they were both living a sort of masquerade. Sure, they went to church, but they never committed their hearts and their lives to Jesus. So late one night, after a youth group meeting at our home, I decided to talk to them. After a quick cookie and a long prayer, I went into the living room and told them about Jesus Christ.

My father was the first to say anything back, and it surprised me. He told me he had asked Christ into his life about 30 years ago, and that only a week ago he had recommitted himself to Christ. I asked him what made him do it, and he said that he had seen what wonders God had done in my life and how I had changed.

My mother was into New Age ideas, and wasn't quite sure of her reaction to what I said.. So as not to force anything on her, I simply gave her a tract and asked her to read it, and suggested that we could talk about it later. A few days passed and I asked her if she had any questions on the tract. She still didn't know if it was right, so I laid off a little while. About a week and a half later, she finally came around and accepted Christ into her life. The miracle of that decision was that Mom had tried many religions and was very frustrated by them. Now she wouldn't be frustrated any longer.

Since then, my father has lost his job, my grandma has become very ill, and we as a family have lost many close friends. But the Lord is bringing us through those trials and tribulations for a reason—to make us stronger as a family. The Lord does everything for a purpose and whatever He is allowing in *your* life, He is doing it because He loves you.

A REASON TO LIVE

I was brought up in a strong Christian home and have always believed in God, but until last year at camp I had never really accepted Him into my heart. I knew He existed…I just didn't really understand completely *why*. But last year I accepted Him into my heart. My life was headed for a serious change, or so I thought.

I did fine with being a Christian at camp, but as soon as I got home my walk with God began to slip. I hung around the kind of people who invite trouble. I began to forget all about God, and turned more toward Satan's side. I began to skip classes and smoke. I let my grades drop and was even kicked out of a few classes. For a girl, that is a sure sign of a rebel! I can remember not being very happy, and fighting with my parents even more.

My best friend at the time was a girl named Mindy. She was a year older than I and really confused. Throughout the year she dated a guy named Frank, and he was serious about her. She was really selfish and literally wanted it all. About halfway through the year she decided she didn't want him anymore, but instead wanted one of my frequent boyfriends, Scott. Well, she dumped Frank, and within days she and Scott were a popular couple. Meanwhile, both Frank and I were hurting really bad. Because of similar feelings, we started spending time together.

Within a few weeks he and I were going steady. We didn't realize that Mindy wasn't done with us, and we blindly went on. Well, Mindy decided she didn't like the way things had turned out, and started to work herself back into Frank's life. He dropped me real quick, and they were once again together forever.

After a while she began to tire of him and tried to get Scott back. He came with no resistance, and Frank was dropped once more. Thinking it would be different this time, Frank and I once again went out. We were wrong. It went on like this for the remainder of the year, and by the end of the year Mindy and I were no longer friends. I tried to stick by her, but soon realized it wasn't working. I'm not trying to be down on Mindy—she really is nice and all, just a little confused.

Well, all this made me realize how stupid I had been and how awful the devil can make you be. When school got out, I quit smoking and hung around totally different people. I began to get my life back together again, but I still hadn't rededicated my life to Jesus.

Finally it was time for camp, and I was really excited. I couldn't wait to see my friends and get my life under control. I got to camp and instantly things started falling into place. With the help of friends, counselors, and the talks I heard, I rededicated my life to Jesus. I began to learn more about God than I had before. I began to read the Bible voluntarily (which I had never done before), and I learned a lot. God really does know how I feel and how life can get. I found that out one day on a camp-out.

I opened my Bible and read Psalms 1, 3, and 5. I really could relate to them, and instantly I knew that God was talking to me. He wanted me to straighten out my life. He wanted *me.* I almost cried. It was so awesome to think about. It still gives me the shivers.

I'm so happy now, so full of joy that I just can't wait to tell my mom and my youth leaders. I know they will be happy for me and join in my joy. I just hope that in some way during the school year I can affect someone else's life and help them know the happiness and peace the Lord can bring. I hope people will see the Lord through me and come to know Him too. I'm just so happy I can't explain it. I have tears in my eyes, yet I'm smiling my mouth off! Our God is truly an awesome God!

CASEY'S STORY

NORMAL AMERICAN KID

I have a friend who had a pretty hard time growing up. No, she wasn't an alcoholic and she wasn't beaten, nor was she on drugs. On the surface she was just a normal American kid. Her parents always provided very plentifully for her. In grade school she succeeded greatly both in academics and socially.

In middle school things began to change. Her friends became more aware of trends and boys. By the sixth grade, she noticed the way her friends gradually started denying their parents' authority. It was really hard growing up with a mother who thought she was perfect, and who always expected my friend to be just like *she* was. My friend can remember being sent back upstairs because a pair of shorts made her hips look too wide or a shirt just didn't look right. She could never satisfy her mother's standards.

By the time she was twelve, she began resenting her mother's attention to her physical appearance. She wanted so badly for her mom to notice how she was changing and maturing on the inside, but her mom never did. The mother was so caught up in the way she wanted her to be, that she never realized how her daughter was self-destructing.

After seeing her friends treating their parents badly and really not communicating within the home, my friend thought that being disrespectful was a cool thing to do. So she began testing her parents' trust. As she drifted away from her parents, she depended more on her friends for support. But a lot of times that support wasn't there. Her friends were more caught up in themselves and their possessions than in helping out someone else.

My friend wanted to be popular and she wanted everyone's attention all the time, so she started to concentrate on the materialistic things of the world. She tried to use the things her parents gave her to win friends at school. She thought that if her mom saw her with the in crowd, and gaining lots of friends, her mom might finally be satisfied with what she had become.

But this never happened. As my friend started focusing

on superficial things of the world, she lost sight of the values and character her parents had instilled deep within her. Her grades began to drop, and her parents' trust was falling daily. She began to lie to her parents to make them momentarily happy, which only kept getting her into more trouble. The friends she had hoped to gain never surfaced, and her parents were more disappointed in her than ever.

My friend was a very unhappy girl. She had tried to find her place, a place where she could satisfy everyone and herself, but something was missing. She felt like she was caught in a trap and the walls were being built higher and higher around her.

I should know...my friend is me.

I denied responsibility for so long that I didn't know where to turn for help, or encouragement, or security. And then one day I found Jesus. I was at a church service at camp, and Michael W. Smith was singing his song "Emily." The words amplified in my heart the way I was feeling: caught in an endless time, waiting for a sign to show me where to go. Insecurity was my life, or my way of life before I accepted Christ.

The greatest feeling I've ever felt is knowing God loves me. I know that no matter what the world thinks of me, I'm faultless in God's eyes. I can be tall, short, fat, or skinny, and God can see straight through that to my heart.

When I started doing things for Christ and not for my parents or friends, I was the happiest person I know. Learning how to satisfy Christ is life's lesson, and I'm trying to learn step by step. Without Christ I was a little brat who could only say, "I want this," "Gimme that," and "Me!" Now I thank God daily for what He's made me, and I pray for His plan for my life.

I'll never forget that Sunday when the biggest burden I've

ever known was lifted off my shoulders and I, by the grace of God, was relieved with a peace of God that is hard to understand (unless you've felt it).

Now I'm closer than ever to my parents, and with God's help I've earned back their trust. As for my friends—well, there aren't as many of those as there used to be, but my most important friend is Jesus.

I encourage you to never tell yourself you're less than you are. With God all things are possible, and I've found a security that will keep me till eternity.

MY FROWN HAS GROWN A SMILE

I've always had a bad attitude toward the world, and have been noncompliant toward authority. But this last year has been especially hard for me. I had at least five really bad arguments with my mom, and a few with my dad. I tried to commit suicide by drinking an entire bottle of cough syrup, and another time I took about a dozen Sudafed at once.

Then I was admitted to a psychiatric hospital for a week. This wasn't a new thing for me. In the past I had been in other psych hospitals two times, once for three months and once for more than a year. I was admitted both times for the same thing: "oppositional behavior," not caring about life, running away, and basic attitude problems.

In 1985 at summer camp I accepted the Lord into my heart, but I haven't walked the walk at all. I started listening to heavy metal and really got into the attitude (which is ter-rible) that went with it. I started with Iron Maiden, Poison, and other glamour bands, then I turned to Metallica, Megadeth, Slayer, etc. It got faster and faster until I got into the Cro-Mags and the Storm Troopers of Death. I also experimented with alcohol, then really got into it. It was a big mistake. I left home for a week and came home to get my tapes and some clothes. I was there when my dad came home, but I left anyway.

I stayed away five more days, going to wild beer parties, etc. One night all of my 85 tapes were stolen. They were all I ever cared about, and I was crushed. I took better care of my tapes than I did of myself. Back home my room was always a wreck, and my bed was never made, but my tapes were always neatly stored in boxes inside drawers.

Then about a week later I went away for two days to a carnival and worked for $15 a day, and just went out at night and partied hard with the other carnies. The day I went home was the Fourth of July. My parents had stopped saying no, because I still went out and partied. It was at that point in my life that they lost all faith in me.

I have never said no to peer pressure because I didn't know how, and I really wanted to learn. On the night of August 12, I got more scared than I've ever been in my life. I had a dream/nightmare in which my house was struck by lightning and demolished. Later in my dream, I was killed by lightning, and a big bolt struck near my cabin and I saw the purest white. I had the most peaceful feeling in my life. I was asking myself if I was dead or alive, and I rededicated my life to Christ.

I have prayed and I will not go back to drinking and heavy metal music. I stay home more, and play a lot more pool and go bowling and do other things with my Christian friends whom I love very much, and who don't make the mistakes I did.

To say things have changed for me is a big understatement. Christ changed *everything* for me. My frown has grown a smile.

12

MORE OUT OF LIFE

His father laughts: "We'd have added another word to his name if we thought of it soon enough," He's looking back over fifteen years as the father of one of America's truly great teenagers: John Wesley Hays White.

Wes, as the boy's friends know him, has what John Wayne called grit. General Patton called it guts. Vince Lombardi called it "the stuff it takes to be a winner." The Bible calls it *endurance*. Wesley White certainly has 'em all. His life story would make a box office smash hit in a Hollywood movie or a bestselling novel at the bookstore. This story is true.

At age one-and-a-half, a Texas doctor discovered diabetes in Wesley's chemistry imbalance. Taking insulin shots daily for the rest of his life isn't something an 18-month-old wants to dream about. But the insulin seizures that were to come were worse than the needle.

As if that weren't enough for one person to bear, when Wes was two-and-a-half another doctor diagnosed a greater complication: Wesley was an epileptic. The two disorders immediately began to trigger each other. During a six-month period of intense hospitalization, Wesley would have seizures (grand mal —the worst kind, with falls and head bruises) as often as one every minute. He wore a hockey helmet in the hospital to protect himself. The doctors told his parents that Wes would never grow up, that he would always be confined, and that there was probably permanent brain damage.

The doctors couldn't have been further from the truth. The problem was that they didn't measure the size of Wesley's heart. That heart began to drive Wesley to becoming not just "normal," but extraordinary.

In sixth grade he took up boxing for a sport. Wes looks back at the next three years in the ring and smiles: "It was a challenge. I liked to go into the ring alone and have to stand up for a few minutes while another guy tried to take me off my feet. I never wanted to destroy the opponent, I just wanted to win." Win is what Wesley often did. He fought his way to the state championships, where he was first runner-up.

Now that Wes is in high school, football is his sport. Never mind the diabetes and epilepsy (still a nagging problem). Wes is only five-foot-five and he weighs 120 pounds. Guess what position he plays? You guessed wrong. Defensive tackle! This year he started on the junior varsity, and played some with the varsity as a sophomore. Facing a 200-pound opponent was not unusual. Wesley has gotten used to big obstacles.

Want to know more? Wes has been a rodeo clown. With his father he would do a funny act in the arena in front of a 2,000-pound Brahman bull who wasn't in on the joke. "I love to see people laugh and have fun," Wes says.

The medical problems continue. When asked why he doesn't lose heart, Wes says humbly, "I just go on. I don't like to sit. You can have fun if you want to. This disease is mine, and I might as well enjoy it and get the best from life."

This summer he enjoyed life in a kayak on one of America's swiftest and roughest whitewater rivers. Who knows what he'll think of next?

"I believe God loves me," Wes concluded. "I believe He is faithful. He's coming back for me. He's my best friend."

I can see why Wesley White is a winner. Pound for pound, given what he's been given, Wes gets more out of life than any young man I know.

MISTI'S STORY

THE "C" WORD

I come from an extremely strong Christian family. My father is a minister, so naturally my mother, older sister, and

I were in church every time the doors were open (literally). I accepted Christ as my personal Savior at the age of five, although I didn't understand the promises for my life until years later.

I spent about the first ten years of my life growing up in a town of about a thousand people in the swamplands of South Carolina. I was a true tomboy and was willing to try anything once—which included beating up all the boys my age. God gave me a strong, healthy body and a good mind that allowed me to breeze through schoolwork.

At the beginning of my seventh-grade year we moved back to Oklahoma, where my parents were originally from. I began to get serious about basketball around this time. (I was already six feet tall at age 11!)

In the ninth grade I was diagnosed as having ovarian cancer. I classified it in my mind along with Algebra I—no big deal. While sitting in the waiting room, wondering what the doctors were going to do, I told my mom that if the doctors came out and told me I only had three weeks to live, it would be all right. (I don't remember saying that, but my mom reminded me about it later. My parents also told me later that hearing their 13-year-old speak those words had given them strength.) God was already beginning to move in my life even at the early stages of my sickness. I was not afraid, somehow having a peace about the sickness. ("Be strong and courageous. Do not be terrified; do not be discouraged, for the Lord your God will be with you wherever you go" —Joshua 1:9.)

The doctors proceeded to do a complete hysterectomy, and they prescribed no follow-up treatment. We praised God that everything went well and that I was safe. I was happy just to be able to play basketball again in five weeks. My busy schedule kept my mind off the cancer. The doctors told us that my kind of cancer would probably recur within two years if it was going to at all. They were right! Exactly two years later, a CAT scan came back positive.

The doctors discovered a large mass on the upper left side of my abdominal wall. Through the grace of God, my family and I were prepared. I think that once you experience something so devastating for the first time, you always expect it to happen again. We gave the burden to God and just looked to Him for guidance ("I can do all things through Him who gives me strength" —Philippians 4:13). Notice that I keep saying "we"; this is something my entire family took part in along with hundreds of other prayer warriors and Christians. I was by no means alone. Not only did I have God, who was ALL I really needed, but I had the fellowship of my Christian family. Doesn't it seem as if we often take for granted that God-provided fellowship?

Back to the C Word: The kind of cancer my body was fighting was lymphatic cancer, which lies in your lymph glands. Due to the fact that it could spring up again anywhere, the doctors chose for me to undergo chemotherapy.

My initial reaction was *Nooooooooo!* Chemotherapy does three things: It breaks up your hair cells (which causes baldness), breaks up your red blood cells (which causes weakness), and breaks up your cancer cells (killing off the disease). Eventually the blood cells and hair cells bond together again, while the cancer cells do not. However, I tried to strike a bargain with God—something I would not advise anyone else to do—and told Him under what circumstances I would accept this burden. I told God that I would accept the sickness and be a happy camper, but under no circumstances would I go bald for Him.

But God's plan had already been set in motion, and I was along for the ride. I had to learn to be submissive to

His will and accept the fact that He knew what He was doing. Looking back now, I realize how little God was asking from me (only my hair!), especially compared to what I had cost Him—His Son's life.

I naturally had to undergo the chemotherapy in order to survive. My treatments were scheduled once a month. By this time I was a hospital veteran, so the needles weren't too bad.

After one of my treatments, I can remember waking up at home and not being able to see, due to an allergic reaction to anti-nausea medication. *This is getting out of hand,* I thought. Wasn't God supposed to make this easy on me since I was accepting the sickness? I was furious with God and proceeded to tell Him so. Yet I also knew that God was my source of strength. I prayed that He would take away my anger and forgive me for not trusting the working of His plan. And He did.

So now, when was I going to lose my hair? It wasn't long! Losing your hair has got to be the grossest of the gross—hair gets on *everything!* Finally, my parents and I sat down in front of the TV, and I proceeded to spread out a sheet, sit down in the middle of the sheet, and pull my hair out. (It was really sorta neat!) What was really amazing was the fact that no one in my family was shocked by having a six-foot-two skinhead running around the house. Ten minutes after losing my hair, my mother joked around with me, asking how I would know where to stop applying my makeup since I had no hairline! God hadn't taken me up on the bargain, but little did I know that later on the loss of my hair would be a big blessing in my life.

Now came the big test: How did I face my friends at school as a bald adolescent? I would face them through God's peace of mind that only He can supply. He promises to take care of us. It was only by God's power that I got up in the morning, put on one of Dad's baseball caps and set off for high school. He gave me the ability to joke about my baldness with the other students so they wouldn't be embarrassed. Besides, now I could sleep later before school since I didn't have to curl my hair!

Isaiah 40:31 tells us that "those who hope in the Lord will renew their strength. They will soar on wings like eagles; they will run and not grow weary; they will walk and not be faint." I had to wonder about this verse when basketball season rolled around. I could barely walk, much less run. Yet God came through as always, providing me with the strength to play in those games. I played the games wearing a painter's cap, mainly because when my scalp began to sweat, my head got cold. Because I was such a visible player (I was also one of the top scorers in the state), the news media wanted to do features on me, mostly due to the fact that I was bald. If I hadn't lost that hair, they wouldn't have been as interested.

What a witnessing tool! Publicity about a Christian! When the reporters came around to the big question—"Misti, how do you do it?"—I was ready with the big answer: "God gives me my strength." When I was able to say that on TV and in newspapers, touching thousands of people with those five words, all the cancer, all the nausea, all the pain, all the lost hair, all the humiliation, all the anger, and all the lost pride was worth it! And I'd do it again!

I went on to speak at many public functions, including one "gig" in front of 7,000 young people at a summer camp. Talk about a mountaintop experience! Although Christ was touching others through me, He was doing some personal work in my life as well, and it made all the tribulations worth it.

I had my last treatment in January, and the doctors say I am cured. However, I could have told them that a long time ago. In my last year in high school I went on to be senior class president, valedictorian, math and science club president, National Honor Society president, Fellowship of Christian Athletes "Athlete of the Year," all-conference basketball MVP, all-state basketball selection, and all-American basketball selection, and I was recruited by over 90 major NCAA Division I schools to play basketball for them.

If those aren't each and every one a blessing from God, I don't know what is! "'For I know the plans that I have for you,' declares the Lord, 'plans to prosper you and not to harm you, plans to give you hope and a future'" (Jeremiah 29:11). My future lies at the University of Kansas at present, and I know that the Lord has many blessings for me here. I look forward to many more trials, as I know they will help me grow closer to our Lord.

13

FOLLOW THE STAR

'm still shivering as I write this. After being lost on an evening solo elk hunt for several hours tonight (coyotes, wolves, no moon, and *all* the trimmings) in a national forest in western Colorado, I've miraculously found this quaint little farmhouse refuge. Baby! You don't know how good it is to be found until you've been lost for real. I had run out of water as I walked half-scared through the darkness, stumbling through gullies, sagebrush, creeks, beaver dams, and my own mental confusion. After I realized I was really (like *really*) lost, I hit my knees and prayed (like billions of times before), "Lord, I've run out of strength. Please get me home."

I looked up and saw a familiar group of stars in the northwest sky. The ancient Greeks called it Cassiopeia's Chair, but we call this handful stars the Flying W, because that's exactly what they look like. (In fact, I used to kid Debbie-Jo when we were dating, as we gazed into the sky on a beautiful summer evening, "Honey, if you'll marry me I'll have your new last initial monogrammed into the sky." She fell for it!)

As I looked at the familiar constellation, I noticed that it was just east of the North Star. A quick memory picture from a map I'd seen told me that civilization was northeast of me. My prayer was answered with the thought, *Follow the W.* (This is not astrology, mind you! Knowing the locations of stars and appreciating their beauty is a far cry from believing they have a mysterious occultic message for our lives today. Please remember that.)

I continued to stumble through the darkness. My pulse was high, but I knew if I didn't leave my course, eventually I'd hit a highway.

A funny thing happened: I hit a small dirt road, and at first I was relieved. After a few hundred feet, however, the road turned northwest. Decision time met me in the face: Take the road, or follow the star.

I followed the star. One hour later I saw a light from the window of this farmhouse. Needless to say, my blistered feet danced a happy song.

It seemed to be life in a microcosm, life for me and for you: All the tears and smiles and victories and defeats and preventions and warnings of this book aligned themselves tonight, coming together in a flow as clear as a Rocky Mountain stream.

Life has sunshiny days and dark, dark nights. God is present when the paths are lit, yes; but He's also present—omnipresent—when it's darker than dark. His word is our guide, lit by His love like a star in the sky. Yes, there are lots of wolves and coyotes around to scare you, and lots of sudden gullies to trip your feet, and alluring paths that look so enticing, yet won't get you safely home. But the net effect of all these things can be to pull you closer to His side.

My young friends in this book are living "happily ever after." They've all decided to follow their Star.

And it's there in the sky for you as well.

ERIC'S STORY

GETTING HIGH

As I hit junior high school a few years ago, I realized I had a whole life to fill up, and my friends and I decided that drugs were the basic ingredients for doing the job. Little did I know that drugs would eat a hole right through me, leaving me emptier than before. Somehow they robbed me of my motivation. I no longer was the ambitious sports collector I had been when I was younger. No longer did I give a flip about school, sports, my parents, or my health. I figured my friends and I would all party together for eternity.

Before long our whole crowd got sick of sitting around in people's rooms getting high with the same old pot. It didn't take long to figure out that pot alone wouldn't cut it. We added cocaine, acid, ludes, and sex to our diet, but still kept getting bored. I made fun of people who I actually admired, because I wanted them to hurt the same way I was hurting. My friends ripped me off, but I didn't say much about it because they ran the show, not me. I wasn't about to get kicked out of my party clique.

I never felt cool except when I put on a good performance, which was always temporary and insufficient for filling my needs. This whole lifestyle somehow absorbed all my motivation. I decided I couldn't fit in anywhere except in a drug scene. I was not good at anything but drugs. I freaked out when people quit partying because that was the only thing I had.

I was sick of hiding, sick of worrying, sick of being paranoid, sick of being a slave to self-consciousness. I wanted to do something, to be somebody: a good athlete, a confident friend. But my present lifestyle had ripped me off. I wanted peace and freedom. I felt so left out. I was trapped in an unsteady, unsturdy world where no trust existed. There was only worry—worry that no relationship was stable, and that I could go down the drain at any time. My whole world depended on what my friends thought of me. I was afraid to be myself, and I hated all of it.

My self-confidence was shot. I knew drugs were making me selfish, sneaky, and guilty, even though I hated being that way. I knew I was becoming uncool. I hated myself for what I had become; therefore, I could accept no love, no compliments, and no responsibility. I had so much guilt that I could only feel sick and lonely and empty. I hated myself for the painful heartaches I had inflicted on my parents each time I got busted by the cops or kicked out of school.

So many people hate what they are doing, but they won't let go of it because it's easier to hate and to be revengeful. It's easier to be ticked off, power-hungry, and greedy. So many people are slaves to self-consciousness. More and more I realized that I had separated myself from God, our Creator. I had separated myself from everything as I searched through drugs, sex, and power. Psalm 100 told me, "Know that the Lord Himself is God. It is He who has made us and not we ourselves; we are His people and the sheep of His pasture."

I've found that God created us, and He knows how to fulfill us. We all have the desire to be high because God didn't make us to sit around and be a drag. Watch the deer spring through the brush; they are full of life! Feel a little puppy lick you all over your face; puppies are full of love. Only our Creator can get us truly high, and fill us with life and love. It happens as we let Him live through us, as we die to our stupid old ways and begin to follow in Jesus Christ's footsteps.

If you've only been high on cocaine and marijuana, then you've never been high. We try to fill ourselves with life, yet we aren't tough enough and cool enough to cut it. Jesus Christ can fill us because He designed us that way. We are to live with God, not apart from Him.

Jesus saved me from the sickest, emptiest, loneliest feeling in the world. My heart is mended, my brain restored, my mind at peace, and my confidence regained. My joy is made full. Trials only turn me into a cooler person than I already am, and my parents are my best friends. I played basketball in high school, got good grades in college, and have friends who will protect my back. I am free! This is the truth. I have been freed!

FREEDOM FROM THE GRIP

I am writing this to help others whom Satan has lied to, and who believe their soul belongs to him. It is terrifying to believe you are totally separated from God and that there's no hope. I am writing my testimony as proof that there *is* hope. Anyone who desires God and fears God has hope. Psychiatrists couldn't help me—only true, caring Christians and God's word helped.

While I was "high", I imagined that Satan asked me to give up the Holy Spirit, and I said yes. I didn't really mean it, but I couldn't help feeling I had blown it with God. I cried and asked for forgiveness and sought counsel, but nothing helped. I had nightmares that Satan was tormenting me.

I couldn't understand why all this had to happen to me. I was mad at God for not protecting me from it. I lived in total fear, was suicidal, and went into depression for two very long years. I had given up! A Christian told me that this awful experience and terrible pain would help others some day, because I would be able to understand their pain.

After so much fear and pain, I finally reached a turning point. I decided that if God had allowed this to happen, it was because He is a mighty, loving God and He would not fail me. I decided I wanted to live. I decided that God was loving and powerful enough to overcome my problems and to prove His love to me. I decided that rather than giving up and facing hell, I would wait for God's mercy. I would wait for Him to show me that I'm okay. Even if I had to live in depression until I was 80 years old, I knew enough about God to believe He would help me some day. This was the beginning of faith.

It was small faith, but it's all I had. Matthew 13:44 says that the Kingdom is like a man who finds a buried treasure and sells all he has to buy the field the treasure is in. God has given all He has to win our will over to Him. We are His treasure. He gave His own life here on earth to suffer as we do, and He died like we will to prove He understands and loves us. The turning point for me, the moment healing really began, was when I stepped out and exercised the little faith I had.

I once thought I was sold to the devil. Now I know I'm a vessel of God. These are the truths and the steps God showed me that saved me:

> **Proverbs 1:7**— *Fear of God is the beginning of the knowledge of God. (I had to fear judgment before I could be saved.)*

> **Matthew 12:20**— *A bruised reed He will not break, a smoldering wick He will not snuff out. (This gave me more hope, because I was a flickering candle. I was hanging on by the skin of my teeth.)*

> **James 2:17**— *Faith without works is dead. (I didn't have much faith, but I started moving forward with what little I had. God needs a little bit to work with. You have a free will, and He won't take over. You have to try a little, and He does the rest.)*

> **Matthew 9:29**— *According to your faith it will be done unto you. (God rewards us according to our faith.)*

Matthew 13:31— *The Kingdom is like a mustard seed…the smallest of seeds becomes the largest of garden plants. (Faith grows and multiplies. You don't have to start out with a whole bunch.)*

Matthew 13:33— *The Kingdom of heaven is like yeast. (Even in a small amount, think what yeast does to the bread.)*

Matthew 17:20— *Have faith like a mustard seed, and you can move mountains.*

Matthew 24:13— *Don't give up! Only those who endure until the end will be saved. (You must fight the fight.)*

Romans 10:17— *Faith comes by hearing, and hearing by the word of God. (Read the Bible, pray for insight from it daily, meditate on it. That is how your faith and your relationship with God will grow.)*

Proverbs 2:1-5— *Search for God as if He were buried treasure.*

All my life I was told to love God with all my heart, but I didn't know Him. How do you love someone you don't know? Fear is the beginning of knowledge of God. First I was afraid that God would send me to hell. Then in my fear and desperation I sought Him. Then I found Him. Now I know God and am getting to know Him better. So what if I thought I had sold out to the devil? That's what scared me into looking for Jesus!

THE NASTY NINE (LESS ONE)

The Nasty Nine started when I was ten years old. I met up with a group of kids like me who had come from broken homes. We started getting together as a club. We called ourselves the Nasty Nine because that was the exact number of us, and we had decided to be just as nasty to the world as it had been to us. The problems in each of our broken homes are too many to describe.

At the early get-togethers we would listen to music groups like KISS, Twisted Sister, Ratt, Van Halen, Culture Club, etc. The music began to support my feelings of hatred, and my perception that there was no God. It also made me think it was all right to drink and smoke pot. We would at first just take a drink of beer and one hit of pot. Then it was a can of beer and a few hits. Then it was shots of tequila or Jack Daniels and a whole joint. It ended up with us getting blitzed and doing coke. I never shot up though, because I'm afraid of needles. The worst thing was that I began to depend on the Nasty Nine for my comfort, security, and the like.

One of the big things about our club was that we didn't believe there was a life after death or a God, even though some of us had been saved. Now we had to prove to ourselves that we weren't afraid to die, by doing dangerous stunts. We would go out and jump off bridges, stand in front of moving cars, and whatever. One time I stood in front of a moving car and was so drunk I wouldn't get out of the way. If it hadn't been for a friend, I would be dead. There are nights that I have no memory of what I did or who I'd been with.

Today, Joe, I heard you speak, and I decided to change all that. I won't be stupid any longer. I am tired of being ashamed and of all the lying and deceit. With God's help, I will become clean. I thank you for helping save my life because I soon would have died.

Today I wrote this letter to the Nasty Nine (less one):

Dear Nasty Eight,
I am writing to inform you that I am going to make a few changes in our "social" club. Since coming to college I have realized that most of our ideas were way off base, so I am not going to party with you anymore. I know this will make most of you mad and you'll consider me a hypocrite. But I'm not. You see, I was a lost sheep of Christ, and now I am found. I wake up in the morning feeling more alive and better than I have since I joined up with you. I hope that some of you can still love me, but be fore-warned: You will love me clean and sober, because that's how I intend to stay. There will be no more drugs, alcohol, or your type of parties for this girl. I will no longer be the Master of Ceremonies or any-thing else. I pray for you.

[Two weeks later, Betty wrote me this...]

So much has happened, Joe, since I last spoke with you. When I went home that night, the Nasty Nine (less one!) were waiting for me; so I read aloud to them the letter I had written. Needless to say, they were not very happy. For some reason they wouldn't believe me. I got real angry and told them all to get out and not come back until they were sober and clean because I wasn't going to do that stuff any more. My boyfriend, who's part of the Nasty Nine, hit me and told me that I was trash just like them (the Nasty Nine), and that no matter how hard I tried I would end up back with them. Then they all left. This scared me. For the first time in over six years I prayed and asked Christ to help me be strong.

Joe, tomorrow it will be two weeks since I spoke with you, and I haven't had a drink or smoked pot or done coke in all that time! It has been really hard but I have managed. I was just lucky I hadn't gotten addicted to the coke!

Since that day I haven't felt lonely once. I know that in time He will heal all of my wounds! Through Him and sobriety I am experiencing so many things like love and beauty in nature and people. It's still a daily struggle for me not to drink and get high, but I know if I keep Him first, it will get easier. The Bible says God will place no burden on me that's too great to bear, so I know I can make it.

[And this came to me later...]

It has been seven months since I last touched a drop of alcohol or did drugs. All that seems like only something I read about, something that happened to someone else— and really, through the grace of God, that *was* someone else. Joe, I haven't faltered one time in my fight to stay clean.

That group called the Nasty Nine is no more. After they gave up trying to win me back they just kind of drifted apart. Two of the group are now going to church with me, and both have been saved! Isn't it amazing what great things God can do if we just pray and believe long enough. I have begun to help in my church with our youth group, and I like to think I make a difference.

14

ALWAYS ON THE LINE

I prayed a lot yesterday as I walked into two school gyms in northwest Arkansas. As I often do (and love to do), I addressed the student body regarding drugs, sex, alcohol, and all the other pitfalls of growing up. I didn't know anyone in the rowdy crowds. Coming in cold to a gymnasium of crazy kids always gives me goosebumps and butterflies.

By God's grace, we had a blast! We laughed a lot, and then got down to the serious business of "This is the only body you'll ever have." The kids were hungry for the truth. I let 'em know Christ was the truth. They ate it up like popcorn at a football game! The looks of loneliness and openness and appreciation haunt me today; I wish I could spend my life with each of those kids.

"Pray at all times in the Spirit," Paul says in Ephesians 6. Prayer changes things. One teacher told me she had been praying for one of yesterday's assemblies for hours. Sometimes I speak to kids and forget to pray, or don't have a good attitude as I pray. Those talks are always a failure; I see it in their faces.

Prayer's more essential to life than oxygen. Nothing helps you when you're hurting like having God to talk to, cry to, and reason with. Nothing gives you courage when you're having a huge temptation like asking, "God, what should I do?"

Too often our prayers fall short of their potential because we really never understood what God had in mind when He invented this incredible communication link between Himself and His people. But the fortunate ones are those who've had the unforgettable experience of seeing what prayer can do...

Kathy was a drug addict. She prayed sincerely...and now she's straight.

Alice was an "easy, do-anything girl." She prayed daily for her reputation. Now she's living in purity, waiting for marriage.

Billy had an amazing temper. He blew up at the drop of a hat. He prayed often about his hot-headedness. Now he's under control.

Sam drank to excess and embarrassment. He feared alcoholism and began to pray. He's been dry for two years.

Bart broke up with Amy. She felt like dying inside. Her Youth for Christ leader told her to pray constantly for peace. As the days went by, she saw God's purpose in what had happened, and peace did come.

Prayer is like having a cellular telephone in your pocket. The red "hold" button is always blinking. God is always on the other end of the line. Just push "line one" and start talking.

Pray about everything! Pray when you're scared. Pray when you're doing great. Pray when you're failing. Pray when you're noble. Pray when you're selfish. But at all times, pray to your Daddy in heaven who not only is the "All-Sufficient One," but also cares for you beyond your wildest dreams.

The mystery of great, effective prayer opened up for me when a very wise man pointed out in the Bible six hurdles that make prayer ineffective. If you'll keep these six hurdles off the track, you'll understand clearly why your prayers get the answers they do.

1. The first hurdle is found in James 4:3— "You ask and do not receive, because you ask with wrong motives, so that you may spend it on your pleasures." A *selfish purpose* in prayer robs prayer of power.

2. The second hurdle is found in Isaiah 59:1-2— "Behold, the Lord's hand is not so short that it cannot save; neither is His ear so dull that it cannot hear. But your iniquities have made a separation between you and your God, and your sins have hid his face from you, so that He does not hear."

Sin hinders prayer. "Search me, O God, and know my heart; try me, and know my anxious thoughts; and see if there be any hurtful way in me" (Psalm 139:23-24).

3. The third hurdle is found in Ezekiel 14:3— "Son of man, these men have set up their idols in their hearts, and have put right before their faces the stumbling block of their iniquity. Should I be consulted by them at all?" *Idols in the heart* cause God to refuse to listen to our prayers. An idol is *anything* that is the supreme object of our affection.

4. The fourth hurdle—the *lack of unselfish generosity*—is found in Proverbs 21:13— "He who shuts his ear to the cry of the poor will also cry himself and not be answered." It is the one who gives generously to others who receives generously from God. "Give, and it will be given to you; good measure, pressed down, shaken together, running over, will pour into your lap. For whatever measure you deal out to others, it will be dealt to you in return" (Luke 6:38).

5. The fifth hurdle is found in Mark 11:25— "And whenever you stand praying, forgive, if you have anything against anyone; so that your Father also who is in heaven may forgive you your transgressions." An *unforgiving spirit* is one of the most common hurdles to prayer.

6. The sixth hurdle to prayer is found in James 1:5-7— "But if any of you lacks wisdom, let him ask of God, who gives to all men generously and without reproach, and it will be given to him. But let him ask in faith without any doubting, for the one who doubts is like the surf of the sea driven and tossed by the wind. For let not that man expect that he will receive anything from the Lord." Prayers are hindered by *unbelief.*

Recently I received a letter from a 12th-grade student after a youth rally. With megawatts it broadcasts the message that following Christ isn't an empty, stained-glass, soft church-pew experience. Yes, Sunday morning in church is great, but listen how "Saturday night-ish" this faith is:

I can feel myself changing greatly every day since I decided to let God run my life. It is truly amazing. I get so excited about life now, it is just unbelievable.

Before I accepted Jesus Christ into my heart, I had a problem with drinking (and other things). My dad is an alcoholic, and my brother is too. Therefore I believed my course in life would follow the same path. I thought there was no way around it. I began to feel really bored with life, and I found myself really dependent on alcohol. At times I would ask Jesus to take me off this earth because I hated it so much. At first I thought drinking was all right. Since I grew up around it, I felt it was just part of life, a necessary part of life. How terribly wrong I was!

I tried to stop drinking after realizing I was putting myself in danger of bodily harm. I told myself I was not going to drink for a month. The first night of that month was one of the toughest struggles I've ever been through. I felt I needed to drink more than anything else. But the second night of that month, I gave in. My strength was not enough to over-come my dependency. I felt like a failure. I knew I could not do it alone.

Later, as a true Christian, I tried to stop again. This time it was different! I asked Jesus to help me with my problem and to show me the way to a happy life, and that is exactly what He did! When I tried to stop drinking the second time, it was one of the easiest things I have ever done. I felt no need whatsoever to have alcohol in my system. It was amazing how much easier it was that second time. (But we both know why it was so easy: because Jesus was in the driver's seat.)

I no longer dislike this earth. The new friends, wonderful times, and all the better ways I look at life are just incredible. I have never been so happy, and this happiness will be growing more and more every day! I know there will be trials, but I also know that whatever comes my way, I'll be able to handle anything with the Lord's help!

HE HEARD MY VOICE

It was a cold Friday night in April when the girls' track van pulled into school. The father of one of the girls asked if anyone needed a ride home, but I assured him my parents would pick me up. I called home and my mom said she would be right there. It would take about fifteen minutes, because my school is located in downtown Dallas. I sat down on a bench to wait with some friends on the team. Someone needed to go to the bathroom, so everyone had to go. I had pulled a muscle in my hip, so I decided to stay and watch everybody's bags.

After they left, I felt unusually alone. I watched cars drive by or people walking across the street. Then it became very quiet. I looked over my shoulder and saw a large man walking toward me. I prayed a small prayer: "God, please let him walk by." But he didn't. He came right up to me, grabbed me, and began beating me in the face with his fists. I cannot explain the horror and shock that came over me. I began to scream like I've never screamed before. He threw me on the ground, and I yelled, "God, help me!" For some reason he let go at that instant and ran away.

I got up and watched him run off. I felt bruises on my face as they began to throb with pain. The pulled muscle in my hip had worsened. I tried to hobble around looking for someone, but there was no one in sight. I kept praying for my parents or coach to come.

Then I saw his shadow. He had come back, and this time he had no mercy. He ran to me and started beating me again. I screamed, "Jesus, help me!" Then in a low voice he said, "Shut up!" His eyes were so evil, and I knew he was possessed. Even so, I kept screaming, for this was my only defense. He was so powerful.

He threw me down and started dragging me by my hair to a darker place. I kept trying to get up, and I knew I was giving him a hard time. He grabbed me and with tremendous force threw me down, and I felt something pop in my hip. He began stomping on my head, but I would not let myself get knocked unconscious. He grabbed my sweat pants and tore them like paper. Fortunately, I still had on my track uniform with spandex shorts underneath. He must have been getting frustrated, for he picked me up and threw me against the wall. He kept beating me and I kept screaming for God to save me.

He now had me pinned against the wall very close to him. I could smell the alcohol on his breath. There was nothing I could do; I was exhausted and in pain.

Just when I knew I could hold him off no longer, he let go of me and ran off. I watched a security guard and another man run after him. Even though he was gone, I continued to scream because I was in shock. I looked up and a dear, small black woman came up to me and hugged me. She assured me I was safe now. She said a prayer out loud and I calmed down. Everyone came at once. My coach and teammates called the police, and when my parents came they took me to the hospital. I couldn't walk because a bone had chipped off my hip, and I had a broken nose. My face was beaten black and blue, and my eyes were swollen shut.

The next day I felt very withdrawn. I was closed off to the world, and I did not really want to talk about what had happened. However, as the days went by, the support I felt from family and friends allowed me to open myself up enough to talk about what had happened. As I talked with others and let them show their love and concern and compassion for me, it helped me open up and not be closed off. This helped my mental wounds begin to heal, even though I was still physically hurt.

God gave me a wonderful peace, and I was just thankful to be alive. I knew God had a purpose in all this, for not only was I drawn closer to Him but the security system at school was greatly improved. I know God had His hand in the whole situation, for He saved me just in time. I was not raped or dead, and I was very thankful for that.

> *"I love the Lord, for He heard my voice; He heard my cry for mercy. Because He turned His ear to me, I will call on Him as long as I live! The cords of death entangled me, the anguish of the grave came upon me; I was overcome by trouble and sorrow. Then I called on the name of the Lord: 'O Lord, save me!' The Lord is gracious and righteous; our God is full of compassion. The Lord protects the simplehearted; when I was in great need, He saved me."* (Psalm 116:1-6)

KRISTA'S STORY

BREAK THE CHAIN

My father is an alcoholic, and my footsteps were following in his—along a path to self-destruction.

There were many hangovers, many late nights, broken bones (broken nose, fractured thumb, fractured elbow), a wrecked car, and lots of throwing up of blood. I was becoming my father; I couldn't change. I thought it was true because I always heard that your parents are your molders; if your parent is an alcoholic, you'll be one too.

So I thought, *What's the use, Krista? You can't change; you're destined to be like your dad. You're destined to drink all the time. So have a good time, have FUN!!!*

So that's what I did—or that's what I thought I was doing, anyway. The night I broke my nose I had a good time, I had fun. But it wasn't the kind of fun that brought happiness. It was the kind of fun that brought an awful hangover, and, along with that, a lot of regret.

But that didn't stop me. I continued to drink. I continued to find my happiness in a bottle. But what happened when I got to the end of the bottle? It was empty, just like my life!

The bottle shattered into a million pieces, and nothing was left: no friends to help me, no one to give me a hand picking up the pieces. There was only a bunch of glass cutting me up inside and out, causing unending pain. I was becoming my father. I was becoming an alcoholic. It was my destiny, I kept telling myself. *So have FUN!*

But it came to the point where I couldn't have the so-called "fun" anymore; it was all so overwhelming. There was only emptiness, confusion, and pain. I often wondered what I was even doing wasting my time trying to have fun. What was my purpose here? What were my goals? I had none. I had no purpose. And the fun...well, it was empty, just like the bottle.

I remember crying night after night, praying that God would take me off this earth. I hated it so much! I hated trying to have fun. I hated my life. I hated everything! At that time I didn't know Jesus. I did not know what it means to have a personal relationship with Him. Yet I prayed that God would take me off this earth. I asked this, not knowing then that He loved me so much that He too was crying when I cried. He was trying to tell me He loved me, but I wouldn't listen. He was trying to tell me to come home to

Him instead of to a bottle of alcohol, a bottle of empty pain. He offered me a heart that would never be empty of love, but I turned away so many times. I turned away from Him and turned to myself, thinking I could make things better.

I tried to stop drinking. It was the hardest thing I've ever tried to do. The voice in the back of my head kept saying, *Give it up, Kris. It's in your genes; you're an alcoholic like your dad. Give it up and just live it up!* So I gave in. The voice was right. I couldn't do it. There was no use.

Shortly after this experience I heard a message about someone else who had a similar problem, someone who had parents who were not perfect and who were doing the wrong things. I heard how this person got away from that, and became free from the bondage of drugs and alcohol; how this person, by God's grace, didn't let her parents' actions control her life. But how could this be true?

Then I heard about my true Father, and how He's the One who molded me. All I had to do was ask Him to take over, to forgive me and to change me into what He wanted me to be, into something He would be proud of. I remember that night like it was yesterday. I was so excited to have this new Father. I remember unzipping my heart and asking Jesus to come in and take over. I remember asking Him to help me with my temptation to drink alcohol, because I didn't want to have that negative trait of my father.

Jesus answered my prayers! He took away the temptation exactly like I asked Him, and I didn't drink after that night. Before it was so hard to quit (or to *try* to quit, anyway); but now, with Jesus holding my hand and in my heart, it was the easiest thing I've ever done.

That night I got off my path of destruction and onto a more narrow path…a path that led home, a home full of never-ending love.

I pray that others don't turn away. That they don't choose a path of destruction, but choose the path of God's grace, the path that He so much wants all of us to take. Your life can change, no matter what has happened in the past or no matter what you believe your future must hold. God can change your direction into the right direction. God has some great plan in store for each and every one of His children. Let God take charge and be the Molder of your life. Let Him mold you into something wonderful!

I'm not trying to tell you that life is easy when you become a Christian…because it's not. As I am writing this, my father is drunk, and he's saying and doing things that hurt me inside. I still cry sometimes at night because of this hurt and pain, but now when I pray, I can thank God that He took me off the path I was traveling and showed me a Father of Love who is always there to hold me, to cry with me, and to tell me, "Krista, it's okay, I love you!" I have faith and hope that my dad as well as the rest of my unsaved family members will soon choose this glorious path.

I thank God I have not been drunk since I became a Christian. And I have had more fun than ever before. But now the fun I have doesn't bring hangovers and regrets; instead it brings happiness and rewards.

I love my life now that Jesus changed it around and filled it with His love and gave me a purpose. There is a purpose for each of us if we only let Jesus take control and take us off the path of destruction. God *can* change lives, I know! He changed mine!

15

TIME TO DECLARE WAR

I just hung up the phone. I'm hollow inside, and my hand is weak as I write. Sixteen-year-old Johnny, from a nearby town, just shot himself over a quarrel with his brothers. (The quarrel would have ended someday. He and his brothers would have grown up and become best friends; but Johnny checked out before he could give growing up a chance.)

Last Wednesday Kristi's father called me. His heart had been shattered when he found some letters indicating Kristi was a lesbian. I know how lonely and sad it will be for all concerned if we don't get her straightened out.

Yes, we're at war. It's not just a "tough time" we live in—it's all-out war. As a teenager you have your own battle today that you can definitely win if you'll fight it right. In World War II our whole nation got involved. Everyone sacrificed. We knew it was life or death, so we helped pushed Hitler all the way back to Berlin. The Nazis couldn't believe the fierce determination this American continent mustered in a few short years to join our Allies in fighting and winning that war.

At first we slept...and the results were tragic. Early on a quiet Sunday morning, December 7, 1941, on a Navy base in a harbor on a small island in the Pacific, a young soldier looked carefully at his radar screen. He saw dots...hundreds of dots. He rushed to his presiding officer. The officer brushed it off: "Don't worry; those are just planes coming in from California." Forty minutes later, Pearl Harbor went up in flames. We lost eight big battleships, hundreds of airplanes, and 2,400 sailors and soldiers—all because one lieutenant was lackadaisical in the face of a real threat of war.

Our junior high, high school, and college friends are fighting hard. It's a Pearl Harbor disaster that keeps repeating itself, and we sit at the radar (now a 25-inch, full-color TV set) and see dots…everywhere.

- Every 9 seconds in North America, a teenager engages in sex.

- Every 23 seconds, one becomes pregnant.

- Every 54 seconds, one has an abortion.

- Every 96 seconds, a teenager contracts a sexually transmitted disease.

- Every 14 months, the number of teenagers with AIDS doubles.

- Nine out of ten high school seniors have used alcohol.

- Four million kids are full-blown alcoholics.

- Each year, one of every eight teenagers tries to kill himself.

To accurately describe the enemy, we can't look to Germany or Japan or Iraq anymore. I wish that's all we had to fight! No, our enemy is described in Ephesians 6:12— "Our struggle is not against flesh and blood, but against the rulers, against the powers, against the world forces of this darkness, against the spiritual forces of wickedness in the heavenly places."

Fortunately, our arsenal is loaded to take the enemy to the cleaners. If you will seriously soak up the following pages and put on the full suit of armor that your Creator has designed for you, you will be able to climb into this battle with all-out determination and anticipation of ending up on the winning side of the scoreboard.

Let's look long and hard at Ephesians 6:13-18.

> *Therefore, take up the full armor of God, that you may be able to resist in the evil day, and having done everything, to stand firm.*

Stand firm, therefore, having girded your loins with truth , and having put on the breastplate of righteousness, and having shod your feet with the preparation of the gospel of peace; in addition to all, taking up the shield of faith with which you will be able to extinguish all the flaming missiles of the evil one. And take the helmet of salvation, and the sword of the Spirit, which is the word of God. With all prayer and petition pray at all times in the Spirit, and with this in view, be on the alert with all perseverance and petition for all the saints.

My shoulders still ache daily from the old tired pair of football shoulder pads I was issued my freshman year at SMU. Freshmen always get what's left over. Those pads looked about a hundred years old, and weren't the high-quality gear players enjoy today. When we'd scrimmage against the varsity (giants), my bones would crack. Twenty years later they're still unmended.

How tragic if we were asked to go into the teenage battlefield of the 90s without good armor! It would be like taking a Volkswagen bug head-on into an 18-wheeler on a freeway at 70 miles per hour!

As you look around you, that's exactly the types of emotional wrecks you and I are witnessing.

BUT—

God has given us the armor with which we can fight and win the battle...

IF

we'll stop and put it on!

"God did not give us a spirit of fear, but of power and love and discipline" (2 Timothy 1:7).

Look at Ephesians 6:18 again. Here's the power.

I have a great friend named Riter, a high school senior. He's a linebacker and running back on our football team, Mr. Ball Stealer in basketball, a first-class shortstop in baseball, and a spiritual leader in our school. Riter has also got a wild streak when he gets on his buddy's hot four-wheeler. As he jumped over ditches and trees and flew through our camp the other night, I stopped him with the smile of admiration I always have for him.

"Riter, do they make helmets for those things?"

"Uh, yes, sir. I've got one right up in my house somewhere."

I pursued his safety. "Do you ever think about putting it on? First tree you hit will feel a little coarse without that helmet."

"You bet!" He flew into the darkness. The next night he had it on.

God's armor is seriously recommended. In fact, it's required. Wearing it is not always convenient, but it's literal survival! You've got to put it on...every day.

In your mind's eye, as you think about the armor of the ancient warrior, notice that there's no armor for the back. Don't be timid and walk away from problems. Stand toe-to-toe and fight like crazy. The enemy is a schemer. He's tricky, crafty, deceitful, counterfeiting, and dishonest. He'll do anything to knock you down. He appears in bottles, rolled-up cigarette paper, condom ads, PG movies, *Playboy* magazines (and *Sports Illustrated* swimsuit issues), TV beer ads, seductive perfumes like Poison and Obsession, and a million other attractive dark corners of life.

He never shows you the tragic end result, but he always makes the next step look great. I mean, no sixteen-year-old wants to be an alcoholic, but just one drink can look so fine when everyone else at the party has a glass. Nobody in his right mind wants to wind up alone in an abortion clinic choosing to take life from a helpless baby, but soft skin and sweet cologne and a big moon outside the foggy window can seem so right when love is in the air.

The adversary is named Satan, and I don't think he's too interested in moving pennies across the table in a candlelit room. His interest is moving you to despair in the darkness of temptation.

It's Friday night. The lights are on the field. The smell of freshly cut Bermuda grass is in the air. The band is playing. The student body is cheering. You're ready to play ball. You know that if you play with all your heart, you have the ability to fight and win. The coach passes out your game uniform. This is your battle gear!

The first piece of armor mentioned in Scripture is the girding of the loins, the belt. It is an essential piece that straps the soldier together. In ancient battles it held the breastplate in place, and kept the sword close to the soldier's side. It represents truth because truth is everything. When I lie to my parents, I begin to crumble. When I lie to myself, I begin to fail. When I lie to God, I begin to fall (hard). *Truth* means integrity. Integrity means integrated. Integrated means having it all together and knit tightly. That's what keeps you from coming apart at the seams when times get hard. Practice being honest about every detail of your life, and your uniform will fit like a glove.

A great fighter always went for the heart. One accurate shot to the heart would surely take an enemy out of the battle. The breastplate protects the heart. The enemy's spear would ricochet off a good metal breastplate rightly worn with knightly valor. The breastplate to you is *righteousness*. It is both a gift from God and a relentless pursuit of our lives. As a gift, righteousness is the way God sees His children. In Christ, you're a perfect 10. You just couldn't be any more special to God.

While hiking in the Rocky Mountains recently, I became thirsty, reached to the ground, and without any fear of contamination ate the crystal-clear snow that had fallen a day or two before. Rocky Mountain snow sparkles with purity. With Jesus in your heart, so do you. But Paul also writes (as God breathed through his pen), "Let us keep living by that same standard to which we've already attained." In other words, God sees us as a 10; righteousness is yours; *so live righteously!* Jesus says to examine everything carefully, and to abstain from every form of evil. If you'll really do that, your heart will stay in a safe place!

Seventeen-year-old Nikki came up to me after a youth rally recently. Happy tears were running down her cheeks. She poured out her heart about her new friend, Kim, and how Kim had befriended her and led her to Christ. Nikki no longer needed her drugs. The void inside her, left by a shaky home, was now filled with something better. Kim had her shoes covered with *the preparation of the gospel*. Her cleats dug deeply into the astroturf of life. Nikki found life. Kim reached a mountaintop in her own life.

Jason is a sophomore in high school. Every Friday morning he gets seven of his friends together for breakfast and gently brings them along in their walk with Christ (I cook sugar-frosted flakes for their breakfast, and watch with excitement). Jason keeps his feet shod with the preparation of the gospel.

Courtney (my eighth-grader) gets her volleyball team together every Thursday morning for a Bible study. She prays diligently for her teammates' spiritual growth. She, too, reaps the rewards of the well-footed soldier.

Your own shoes are right over there in your closet, just a prayer away. You'll be amazed who they'll lead you to.

Jamie (my 15-year-old) is a cheerleader for our high school. Because of her five years in gymnastics, she has powerful enough shoulders to be a base for her cheerleading squad's pyramid. Her best buddy, Kym, is lightweight and agile, so she goes to the top of every pyramid. Through hundreds of repetitions, Jamie has thrown and caught Kym in a basket throw (high-V sit position) impressively enough to get the squad into the state finals. Kym goes all-out toward the clouds because her best friend, Jamie, whom she has total faith in, is there to catch her.

Two weeks ago, during a highly spirited game, the inevitable happened: Jamie and her base partner slipped. Kym fell through and hit the ground. After a while she was okay. But her faith in her base wasn't. There was absolutely no love lost between these two great friends, but the trick was history. When all-out faith is gone, power is also gone; I can't blame Kym in the least. Grips do slip...but without faith, double stunts don't fly!

"Without faith it's impossible to please God," the Bible says. *Faith* is the mobile shield God gives you to protect any area of your body, mind, or soul from the enemy's flaming arrows.

Ray Utley loves his 7-year-old, Lee, with all his fatherly heart. One summer here at Kanakuk Kamp, Ray was driving a ski boat on a cold Ozarks lake, Lee was riding inside, and a large athlete was slalom-skiing behind. When the athlete made a brisk cut across the lake, he actually flipped the boat and threw Ray and Lee into the cold water. Ray swam frantically around the boat for minutes that seemed like hours, looking for his frail, precious son. His son was nowhere to be found. In one final act of desperation, Ray ducked under the boat and popped up into the 12-inch air pocket formed beneath the deck of the boat. His eyes met Lee's nose to nose, as Lee treaded water waiting for the rescue. Lee looked into his daddy's astonished eyes and simply said, "I knew you'd be here, Daddy."

Faith is believing that God is...*everything*. As one dear old country preacher once said, God may not get there when you want Him to, but He'll be there right on time.

Faith is jumping in your car and zipping down the road with total trust that Goodyear did their job and the tires won't fall off the wheels.

Faith is slamming down a couple of eggs for breakfast without worrying about whether your mom left eggshells in the yolk.

Faith is driving across a bridge without getting out to check with the engineers to see if they put steel bars in the concrete.

Faith is simple; you use it every day! But *by far* the most important faith is the faith you exercise when you say, "God, I believe in you."

The aerobic movement was started by my good friend, Dr. Ken Cooper. Aerobics build your heart when you stretch yourself by running, biking, swimming, or other vigorous exercise.

Faith-aerobics were probably invented by someone like Noah when he was building that huge boat on dry, sunny afternoons in summer. Or maybe they were invented by a scrawny kid named David when he walked into the valley with a dinky slingshot and five small stones, and faced a guy who looked like Kareem Abdul Jabar with a curving, six-foot sword in his hand.

Faith-aerobics are essential. You gotta practice them every day to get in shape for spiritual battle. Your buddy says, "Drink this beer." You say to yourself, *No, God has a super plan for my life and it doesn't include an alcohol habit.* Your mom says to be in at midnight, and everybody else comes in at one. Your emotions tell you to lie, but faith says, *In the long run, God will reward the person who honors his parents.*

The doctor diagnoses a disease in your body. Faith-aerobics go to work as you trust God to heal you on His schedule.

Everyone goes out on Saturday night but you. If you partied more, you could get a date too. Faith-aerobics happen to you when you believe that your body is a temple of God, and that your future husband or wife won't appreciate a used body, and therefore you stay home and believe God for the best.

Faith is probably the single most powerful thing available to you today in all of creation. In last week's mail, a high school junior from Pennsylvania said something that really hits home about this gold mine called faith.

My new relationship with Christ is helping me so much in getting over my depression and the hurt from my dysfunctional family. My father is moving in a couple of weeks and I'm struggling with this. I'm really hurt and angry, but I keep telling myself that my real Father someday will come back and take me to a place where I'll never hurt again. Joe, it's neat to know that even when our parents hurt us and reject us, God is always there to help us deal with our feelings and to hold us up.

The greatest faith of all comes when you get on your knees and say, "God, You can run my life a lot better than I can. I give it up to You. Come into my heart and take over. Here are the keys to my life. You be the driver. I can't do it alone anymore."

That's what ties the faith shield to the helmet of salvation. Kayakers wear helmets. Mountain-bikers wear helmets. Race-car drivers wear helmets. No soldier would dare hit the front lines without one. Yours is a *dependence on God's saving grace* and a total giving of your life into His hands. Christ died on the cross for you. Accepting that gift puts a helmet of protection on your head now and a crown of life to lead you into God's eternal paradise. There's no day like today to try yours on for size.

"And take the sword of the Spirit, which is the word of God" (*Ephesians 6:17*).

"The sword."—If Paul had written that today, he might have called it "the guided missile." And yet a nuclear warhead is far less powerful than the sword Paul was talking about. It doesn't

break the sound barrier—it brings down barriers between kids and parents, teenagers and God, boyfriends and hurt girlfriends.

The sword of God's word changes my life daily, and others too. It calms the 23-year-old drug addict, erases the huge guilt scars to enable the 15-year-old to want to live again, and rebuilds a family relationship for the tenth-grader who ran away from his dad.

Imagine what it would be like if you were on a basketball team that played only defense. Every time you brought a rebound down off the boards or intercepted a pass, you gave the ball back to your rivals and set up your defense. The other team may not score a lot, but you can be sure of one thing: They'll score a lot more than you will!

All the other weapons in your Ephesians 6 arsenal are *defensive* weapons. The sword puts you on the *offensive!* Believe me, you've got to play good defense to live, but the sword enables you to score. God's word is "a lamp unto my feet and a light to my path" (Psalm 119:105). Once you get into it on a daily basis, you'll never put it down.

When Jesus was hit by Satan with some serious temptations, He simply quoted Scripture that was on His heart, and Satan took off with his tail between his legs.

> *"For the word of God is living and active, and sharper than any two-edged sword, and piercing as far as the division of soul and spirit, of both joints and marrow, and able to judge the thoughts and intentions of the heart." (Hebrews 4:12)*

When a guy gets into a tempting situation with a girl, nothing can get him out but a focus on God's word. It always changes your heart. If you've been tempted to look on someone else's paper for answers on a test, let your mind look to God's word and watch your motivation change from the inside out.

Yesterday a 15-year-old high school girl called me, ready to check out on life. She had an abortion last year and couldn't escape the hurt and guilt. Then last spring she was misled again. Her home is pitiful. Her world is coming to an end. As we talked on the phone, I gave her a lot of reassurance and some verses from God's word that have helped me in my troubled times. I can't totally explain it, but while I was sharing verses like Romans 8:1 with her—"There is therefore now no condemnation for those who are in Christ Jesus"—and talking about the true meaning of love, her heart changed. I felt a peace in her voice and a calming in her spirit. She saw God differently. She saw herself differently. She saw life differently. We prayed together. She promised me she'd never kill herself, no matter what happened.

Have you ever had consistent daily quiet times? Have you ever memorized Bible verses on a daily basis? If you get started, look out! Things will begin to change in your life. Those gray clouds that loom in your sky will be overtaken by blue skies like you've never seen before!

A while ago I was at the University of Mississippi recruiting college athletes for our summer camp staff. We were playing a pickup game of basketball on campus when a giant of a man (a running back from the Ole Miss football team) sat next to me. His name was Johnny Boatman. What a fine-looking talent he was. I introduced myself and began to converse with Johnny. Little did I know that the events that followed would change his life forever and develop a friendship between us that I'd cherish for as long as I live. This handsome black man didn't know the Savior. His life was pretty wild, and he was unhappy about it.

I was memorizing Romans 6 that day, and as we talked, I quoted some of it to him.

His eyes opened with excitement. He began to ask questions about God. He had a hunger to know the truth. Later that night, Johnny asked Jesus into his heart. His life turned upside down. Everything began to change for him—girls, parties, sports, studies...everything. The next summer we worked together. I asked Johnny why he was so open to the Lord that day we met on the basketball court.

He told me an amazing story. When he was a little boy he stayed with his aunt a lot. She was a great friend to him, and when he was at her home she would make him memorize Bible verses. Although those days were now fifteen years behind him, Johnny told me that the verses had stayed on his mind and had always drawn him back to the Lord.

When I visited Ole Miss the next year, Johnny was waiting for me. This time he had a friend with him, a talented defensive back on the football team. Johnny had been sharing Christ with this guy and he wanted me to lead him to a personal relationship with the Savior. The defensive back was ready; his heart was open to the Lord. Johnny continues to share his faith in God.

The word of God never ceases to revolutionize lives.

The following plan is a simple program that my friend Bruce Morgan and I call *First and Ten*. It's a way for you to take ten minutes first thing in the morning and spend it with God. Not only will it get your day started off on the right foot, it will give you the offense you need to win the war that surrounds you in your teenage years.

Tonight before bed or tomorrow morning, do lesson one. You'll be amazed at how relevant and practical God's word is.

Get ready for some real fun. Each day complete another lesson, until you have a habit developed.

Ready for action? Here's the plan:

Prayer— Open each time with prayer. Simply touch on the following:

1. *Praise*—Tell God how wonderful He is.

2. *Thanksgiving*—Thank Him for all He's done for you.

3. *Requests*—Bring your needs and cares to Him. Ask Him for things that are important to you.

4. *Preparation*—Ask God to make your quiet time a great one. Here's a prayer from Psalm 119:18—"Open my eyes that I might see wonderful things in your law."

Playbook— That's the Bible. Open it up, read a few verses or a chapter, and think about what it says and what it means.

Observation— Apply your best thinking by bombarding the verse or passage with questions like these:

What is it saying?

What's going on in this passage?

What's the author's point and purpose here?

Who are the people in this passage?

Why is this verse important?

Application— Specifically, what does this verse or passage mean to ME? Consider these questions:

What thoughts come to my mind about my personal life, habits, and attitudes, as I think about this verse or passage?

How can this verse or passage affect my life today?

What changes can come in my life if I really understand this verse?

What convictions does this verse build up inside of me?

Commitment— What will I do about it?

Today, how will I use this verse or passage to make me u better Christian?

What specific goal can I set because of what I've read?

What commitment (promise) can I make to God because of what this passage is saying to me?

On the following pages are some daily guides (a full month's worth) to get you started. Use them, then make up your own. Get a small notebook and keep your own journal of quiet times.

Now ... let the games begin!

Day of the Week: _____ *Date:* _____

THE POWER OF YOUR INFLUENCE

Prayer Requests, Praises, & Thanks:

Playbook: 1 Timothy 4:12—
> *Don't let anyone look down on you because you are young,*
> *but set an example for the believers in speech, in life, in love,*
> *in faith and in purity.*

Observations:

Application & Commitment:

Day of the Week: _____   *Date:* _____

WARNING! WARNING!

Prayer Requests, Praises, & Thanks:

Playbook: 1 John 2:15-17—
> *Do not love the world or anything in the world. If anyone loves the world, the love of the Father is not in him. For everything in the world—the cravings of sinful man, the lust of his eyes and the boasting of what he has and does—comes not from the Father but from the world. The world and its desires pass away, but the man who does the will of God lives forever.*

Observations:

Application & Commitment:

Day of the Week: _____ *Date:* _____

WHO IS JESUS?

Prayer Requests, Praises, & Thanks:

Playbook: John 14:6-7—

> *Jesus answered, "I am the way and the truth and the life. No one comes to the Father except through me. If you really knew me, you would know my Father as well. From now on you do know him, and have seen him."*

Observations:

Application & Commitment:

Day of the Week: _____ *Date:* _____

DO YOU BELIEVE THIS?

Prayer Requests, Praises, & Thanks:

Playbook: John 11:25-26—
> *Jesus said to her, "I am the resurrection and the life. He who believes in me will live, even though he dies; and whoever lives and believes in me will never die. Do you believe this?"*

Observations:

Application & Commitment:

Day of the Week: _____ *Date:* _____

KEEP YOUR EYE ON THE PRIZE

Prayer Requests, Praises, & Thanks:

Playbook: Hebrews 12:1-2—

> *Therefore, since we are surrounded by such a great cloud of witnesses, let us throw off everything that hinders and the sin that so easily entangles, and let us run with persever- ance the race marked out for us. Let us fix our eyes on Jesus, the author and perfecter of our faith, who for the joy set before him endured the cross, scorning its shame, and sat down at the right hand of the throne of God.*

Observations:

Application & Commitment:

Day of the Week: _____ *Date:* _____

RUN TO WIN

Prayer Requests, Praises, & Thanks:

Playbook: 1 Corinthians 9:24—

> *Do you not know that in a race all the runners run, but only one gets the prize? Run in such a way as to get the prize.*

Observations:

Application & Commitment:

Day of the Week: _____ *Date:* _____

WHAT TO THINK ABOUT TODAY

Prayer Requests, Praises, & Thanks:

Playbook: Philippians 4:8—
> *Finally, brothers, whatever is true, whatever is noble, whatever is right, whatever is pure, whatever is lovely, whatever is admirable—if anything is excellent or praiseworthy—think about such things.*

Observations:

Application & Commitment:

Day of the Week: _____ Date: _____

JUDGING OTHERS

Prayer Requests, Praises, & Thanks:

Playbook: Matthew 7:1-3—

> *Do not judge, or you too will be judged. For in the same way you judge others, you will be judged, and with the measure you use, it will be measured to you. Why do you look at the speck of sawdust in your brother's eye and pay no attention to the Plan k in your own eye?*

Observations:

Application & Commitment:

Day of the Week: _____ *Date:* _____

SERIOUS ANGER

Prayer Requests, Praises, & Thanks:

Playbook: Matthew 5:21-22—
>*You have heard that it was said to the people long ago, "Do not murder, and anyone who murders will be subject to judgment." But I tell you that anyone who is angry with his brother will be subject to judgment.*

Observations:

Application & Commitment:

Day of the Week: _____ *Date:* _____

TRUE HAPPINESS

Prayer Requests, Praises, & Thanks:

Playbook: Matthew 5:3-6—
> *Blessed are the poor in spirit, for theirs is the kingdom of heaven. Blessed are those who mourn, for they will be comforted. Blessed are the meek, for they will inherit the earth. Blessed are those who hunger and thirst for righteousness, for they will be filled.*

Observations:

Application & Commitment:

Day of the Week: _____ *Date:* _____

HOW NEW ARE YOU?

Prayer Requests, Praises, & Thanks:

Playbook: 2 Corinthians 5:17—
    *Therefore if anyone is in Christ, he is a new creation; the old
    has gone, the new has come!*

Observations:

Application & Commitment:

Day of the Week: _____ *Date:* _____

GOOD FRUIT

1. Prayer Requests, Praises, & Thanks:

Playbook: Galatians 5:19-23—
> *The acts of the sinful nature are obvious: sexual immorality, impurity and debauchery; idolatry and witchcraft; hatred, discord, jealousy, fits of rage, selfish ambition, dissensions, factions and envy; drunkenness, orgies, and the like. I warn you, as I did before, that those who live like this will not inherit the kingdom of God. But the fruit of the Spirit is love, joy, peace, patience, kindness, goodness, faithfulness, gentleness and self-control. Against such things there is no law.*

Observations:

Application & Commitment:

Day of the Week: _____ *Date:* _____

ALL YOUR NEEDS

Prayer Requests, Praises, & Thanks:

Playbook: Philippians 4:19—
> *And my God will meet all your needs according to his glorious riches in Christ Jesus.*

Observations:

Application & Commitment:

Day of the Week: _____ *Date:* _____

YOUR BODYGUARD

Prayer Requests, Praises, & Thanks:

Playbook: Deuteronomy 31:6—
> *Be strong and courageous. Do not be afraid or terrified because of them, for the Lord your God goes with you; he will never leave you nor forsake you.*

Observations:

Application & Commitment:

Day of the Week: _____ *Date:* _____

WHAT TO DO IN THE FACE OF TEMPTATION

Prayer Requests, Praises, & Thanks:

Playbook: 2 Timothy 2:22—
> *Flee the evil desires of youth, and pursue righteousness,*
> *faith, love and peace, along with those who call on the Lord*
> *out of a pure heart.*

Observations:

Application & Commitment:

Day of the Week: _____ *Date:* _____

GOD'S REMEDY FOR SIN

Prayer Requests, Praises, & Thanks:

Playbook: 1 John 1:8-9—
> *If we claim to be without sin, we deceive ourselves and the truth is not in us. If we confess our sins, he is faithful and just and will forgive us our sins and purify us from all unrighteousness.*

Observations:

Application & Commitment:

Day of the Week: _____ *Date:* _____

WHAT MOTIVATES YOU?

Prayer Requests, Praises, & Thanks:

Playbook: Colossians 3:23-24 —
> *Whatever you do, work at it with all your heart, as working for the Lord, not for men, since you know that you will receive an inheritance from the Lord as a reward. It is the Lord Christ you are serving.*

Observations:

Application & Commitment:

Day of the Week: _____ *Date:* _____

GOD'S 911 NUMBER

Prayer Requests, Praises, & Thanks:

Playbook: 1 Corinthians 10:13—

No temptation has seized you except what is common to man. And God is faithful; he will not let you be tempted beyond what you can bear. But when you are tempted, he will also provide a way out so that you can stand up under it.

Observations:

Application & Commitment:

Day of the Week: _____ *Date:* _____

JESUS UNDERSTANDS

Prayer Requests, Praises, & Thanks:

Playbook: Hebrews 4:15-16—

For we do not have a high priest who is unable to sympa-thize with our weaknesses, but we have one who has been tempted in every way, just as we are—yet was without sin. Let us then approach the throne of grace with confidence, so that we may receive mercy and find grace to help us in our time of need.

Observations:

Application & Commitment:

Day of the Week: _____ *Date:* _____

WHERE'S YOUR FOUNDATION?

Prayer Requests, Praises, & Thanks:

Playbook: Luke 6:47-49—

> *I will show you what he is like who comes to me and hears my words and puts them into practice. He is like a man building a house, who dug deep and laid the foundation on rock. When a flood came, the torrent struck that house but could not shake it, because it was well built. But the one who hears my words and does not put them into practice is like a man who built a house on the ground without a foundation. The moment the torrent struck that house, it collapsed and its destruction was complete.*

Observations:

Application & Commitment:

Day of the Week: _____ *Date:* _____

WHO DO YOU LOVE?

Prayer Requests, Praises, & Thanks:

Playbook: Matthew 5:43-47—

You have heard that it was said, "Love your neighbor and hate your enemy." But I tell you: Love your enemies and pray for those who persecute you, that you may be sons of your Father in heaven. He causes his sun to rise on the evil and the good, and sends rain on the righteous and the unrighteous. If you love those who love you, what reward will you get? Are not even the tax collectors doing that? And if you greet only your brothers, what are you doing more than others? Do not even pagans do that?

Observations:

Application & Commitment:

Day of the Week: _____ *Date:* _____

BITING YOUR TONGUE

Prayer Requests, Praises, & Thanks:

Playbook: James 3:5-6—

> *The tongue is a small part of the body, but it makes great boasts. Consider what a great forest is set on fire by a small spark. The tongue also is a fire, a world of evil among the parts of the body. It corrupts the whole person, sets the whole course of his life on fire, and is itself set on fire by hell.*

Observations:

Application & Commitment:

Day of the Week: _____ Date: _____

WHEN BAD THINGS HAPPEN
TO GOOD PEOPLE

Prayer Requests, Praises, & Thanks:

Playbook: Romans 5:3-5—

We also rejoice in our sufferings, because we know that suffering produces perseverance; perseverance, character; and character, hope. And hope does not disappoint us, because God has poured out his love into our hearts by the Holy Spirit, whom he has given us.

Observations:

Application & Commitment:

Day of the Week: _____ *Date:* _____

THE GATORADE FOR CHRISTIANS

Prayer Requests, Praises, & Thanks:

Playbook: Isaiah 40:29-31—
> *He gives strength to the weary and increases the power of the weak. Even youths grow tired and weary, and young men stumble and fall; but those who hope in the Lord will renew their strength. They will soar on wings like eagles; they will run and not grow weary, they will walk and not be faint.*

Observations:

Application & Commitment:

Day of the Week: _____ *Date:* _____

YOUR ENERGY SOURCE

Prayer Requests, Praises, & Thanks:

Playbook: John 15:4-5—

> *Remain in me, and I will remain in you. No branch can bear fruit by itself; it must remain in the vine. Neither can you bear fruit unless you remain in me. I am the vine; you are the branches. If a man remains in me and I in him, he will bear much fruit; apart from me you can do nothing.*

Observations:

Application & Commitment:

Day of the Week: _____ *Date:* _____

GOD'S DISHES

Prayer Requests, Praises, & Thanks:

Playbook: 2 Timothy 2:20-21—

> *In a large house there are articles not only of gold and silver, but also of wood and clay; some are for noble purposes and some for ignoble. If a man cleanses himself from the latter, he will be an instrument for noble purposes, made holy, useful to the Master and prepared to do any good work.*

Observations:

Application & Commitment:

Day of the Week: _____ *Date:* _____

WHO ARE YOU LIVING FOR TODAY?

Prayer Requests, Praises, & Thanks:

Playbook: Philippians 1:20-21—
*I eagerly expect and hope that I will in no way be ashamed,
but will have sufficient courage so that now as always
Christ will be exalted in my body, whether by life or by
death. For to me, to live is Christ and to die is gain.*

Observations:

Application & Commitment:

Day of the Week: _____ *Date:* _____

GAME PLAN 28
LOOK TO GOD

Prayer Requests, Praises, & Thanks:

Playbook: Luke 11:9-10—
> *So I say to you: Ask and it will be given to you; seek and you will find; knock and the door will be opened to you. For everyone who asks receives; he who seeks finds; and to him who knocks, the door will be opened.*

Observations:

Application & Commitment:

Day of the Week: _____ *Date:* _____

HIDING FROM GOD?

Prayer Requests, Praises, & Thanks:

Playbook: Genesis 3:9-10—
   But the Lord God called to the man, "Where are you?" He
   answered, "I heard you in the garden, and I was afraid
   because I was naked; so I hid."

Observations:

Application & Commitment:

Day of the Week: _____ *Date:* _____

WHEN YOU DON'T UNDERSTAND

Prayer Requests, Praises, & Thanks:

Playbook: Romans 8:28—
> *And we know that in all things God works for the good of those who love him, who have been called according to his purpose.*

Observations:

Application & Commitment:

Day of the Week: _____ *Date:* _____

HOW TO LIVE WITH OTHERS

Prayer Requests, Praises, & Thanks:

Playbook: Ephesians 4:1-3—

As a prisoner for the Lord, then, I urge you to live a life worthy of the calling you have received. Be completely humble and gentle; be patient, bearing with one another in love. Make every effort to keep the unity of the Spirit through the bond of peace.

Observations:

Application & Commitment:

MORE "FIRST & TEN" GAME PLAN SCRIPTURES

To continue your Game Plans, look up in your Bible any of the key verses shown below. Use your own notebook to follow the same format used on the previous pages. As you look up a Scripture passage each day, record on your paper the following three things:

Prayer Requests, Praises, & Thanks

Observations (about the passage you read)

Application & Commitment

The Mystery Uncovered— *Colossians 1:24-27*
Your Responsibility to God— *1 Peter 4:3-5*
You're Free!— *Romans 8:1*
Your Companions— *Proverbs 13:20*
Something that Lasts— *Isaiah 40:8*
Are You Witnessing in Your City?— *Acts 1:8*
The Reason for Sacrifice— *1 John 3:16*
Give It to God— *Philippians 4:6-7*
The Big Love— *Matthew 22:37-40*
Unlimited Ability to Do What's Right— *Philippians 4:13*
When Times Get Rough— *James 1:2-3*
Singleness of Purpose— *Philippians 3:13-14*
The Importance of Obedience— *1 John 2:3-4*
God's View of Parents— *Ephesians 6:1-3*
About that Alcohol— *Proverbs 20:1*
Keeping Your Way Pure— *Psalm 119:9-10*
Stay Hot— *Revelation 3:15-16*
The Greatness of God's Forgiveness— *Psalm 103:11-13*
Real Friendship— *Proverbs 17:17*
Let Him Lift You Up— *1 Peter 5:6*
His Death for Us Foretold— *Isaiah 53:5-6*
Who Do You Listen To?— *Proverbs 3:5-6*
Quality Living— *John 10:10*
Do Others See Jesus in You?— *Matthew 10:32-33*

The Place to Invest Your Best— *Matthew 6:19-21*
God Knows and God Values— *Matthew 10:29-31*
God's Great Love— *John 3:16*
How Much Do You Give God?— *Luke 21:1-4*
Your Salvation— *Ephesians 2:8-10*
What Do Others See In You?— *Matthew 5:16*
Action Love— *1 John 3:18*
Love Will Find a Way— *1 Corinthians 13:4-8*
Belief and Conviction— *2 Timothy 1:12*
Victory Over the World— *1 John 5:4-5*
Equipment for life— *2 Timothy 3:16-17*
Feel Like You Stand Alone?— *2 Timothy 4:16-18*
God's Will for You— *1 Thessalonians 4:3-5*
God's Will for You— *1 Thessalonians 5:16-18*
Contentment— *Hebrews 13:5*
Peer Pressure Release— *Galatians 5:1*
Self-Righteousness— *Luke 18:9-14*
Great Tune!— *Colossians 3:16*
What Directs Your Path?— *Psalm 119:105*
Your Choice— *Romans 10:9-10*
Are You a Good Example?— *Titus 2:7-8*
Your Sustainer— *Psalm 55:22*
When You're Weak— *2 Corinthians 12:8-10*
Real Love— *Romans 12:9-10*
Someone Tell Seventeen Magazine— *Proverbs 31:30*
Where Do You Find Refuge?— *Psalm 71:1-3*
Why Seek Spiritual Knowledge?— *Proverbs 1:1-7*
One God, Our God— *Isaiah 45:5*
Are You Ready to Work?— *Matthew 9:37-38*
What's Hidden in Your Heart?— *Psalm 119:11*
The Prize — *2 Timothy 4:8*
Is Your Light Bright or Dim?— *Philippians 2:14-16*
Who's In Control?— *Proverbs 19:21*
Skeletons in Your Closet?— *Psalm 90:8*
Healthy Fear— *Proverbs 14:26-27*

WHERE TO READ IN THIS BOOK
ABOUT THESE TOPICS:

ABORTION	*Suzette's story*	page 21
ABUSE, EMOTIONAL	*Steve's story*	19
ALCOHOL	*Krista's story*	145
	Sandi's story	61
	Steve's story	19
ANOREXIA/BULIMIA	*Cathi's story*	74
	Cindy's story	107
ASSAULT	*Amy's story*	143
BROKEN RELATIONSHIPS	*Laura's story*	45
CANCER	*Kara's story*	98
	Misti's story	122
DEATH OF A LOVED ONE	*Aaron's story*	63
	David's story	106
DEPRESSION	*Jolene's story*	83
DRUGS	*April's story*	81
	Corey's story	66
	Eric's story	130
	Kathy's story	11
	Linda's story	31
	Nathan's story	17
FRIENDS	*Beth's story*	59
	Mike's story	58

HOMOSEXUALITY	*Rob's story*	page 78
LEARNING DISABILITY	*Angie's story*	99
MENTAL ILLNESS	*Joel's story*	94
PARENTS	*Alma's story*	72
	Brett's story	113
	Brooke's story	68
	Jill's story	88
PEER PRESSURE	*Betty's story*	135
	Erin's story	115
	Paige's story	15
REBELLION	*Bill's story*	119
REJECTION	*Christina's story*	53
ROCK MUSIC	*Nathan's story*	17
SATANISM	*Ann's story*	133
	Paige's story	15
SELF-ESTEEM	*Casey's story*	117
	Janna's story	102
SEX	*Eddie's story*	16
	Kevin's story	31
	Linda's story	31
	Missy's story	30
SUICIDE	*Laura's story*	45
UNSTABLE HOME	*Kristy's story*	65